Practicing for Today's Tests

TIME FOR KIDS

Level 2 Mathematics

Author
Melissa Callaghan

Introduction Author

Stacy Monsman, M.A.

Consultant

Donna Ventura, M.A.Ed.

Publishing Credits

Corinne Burton, M.A.Ed., *President*;
Emily R. Smith, M.A.Ed., *Content Director*;
Angela Johnson, MFA, M.S.Ed., *Editor*;
Johnson Nguyen, *Multimedia Designer*;
Valerie Morales, *Assistant Editor*

Image Credits

Noted graphics and visuals provided by *TIME FOR KIDS. TIME FOR KIDS* and the *TIME FOR KIDS* logo are registered trademarks of TIME Inc.

All other images are from Shutterstock.com, unless otherwise noted.

Standards

© Copyright 2016. National Governors Association Center for Best Practices and Council of Chief State School Officers. All rights reserved.

Shell Education

A division of Teacher Created Materials
5301 Oceanus Drive
Huntington Beach, CA 92649-1030

www.tcmpub.com/teachers
ISBN 978-1-4258-1556-1
© 2016 Shell Educational Publishing, Inc.

Table of Contents

Today's Next Generation Tests

> "Life is good for only two things: discovering mathematics and teaching mathematics."
>
> —Simeon Poisson

Interestingly enough, the French mathematician, Simeon Poisson, does not mention testing mathematics! However, math teachers everywhere realize that tests of mathematics are a reality. And a new reality emerges in today's next generation tests. A pressing challenge is finding high-quality resources that push students with more rigorous problems. *TIME FOR KIDS: Practicing for Today's Tests* answers this very call. It incorporates the rigor of current mathematics standards, the organization of mathematical strands, and higher-level thinking demands of next generation tests into an easy-to-use resource.

What's Different about Today's Standards?

Due to wide variance in standards, a desire for coherence and clear ideas of what math education looks like at each grade level has been a continually evolving process. In 1989, the National Council of Teachers of Mathematics (NCTM) produced *Curriculum and Evaluation Standards for School Mathematics*. Then, NCTM followed up with their powerful document, *Principles and Standards for School Mathematics*, in 2000. Both focus on math content organized by strands and the higher-level thinking skills necessary for true mathematical understanding. *Adding It Up: Helping Children Learn Mathematics* (2001), from the National Research Council, echoes the need for clarity in math education, addressing the problem-solving and reasoning processes applicable to all math content and necessary for conceptual understanding. NCTM's *Curriculum Focal Points for Prekindergarten through Grade 8 Mathematics* (2006) is another noted document in this quest for unifying standards and identifying seminal math topics with a laser-eyed focus. All this

history influences our present sets of standards at the national and state levels (O'Connell and SanGiovanni 2013).

What all of the new standards have in common is a focus on understanding mathematics better. This is achieved through fewer but more rigorous standards that are aligned with college and career expectations. They are internationally benchmarked while also building upon the strengths and lessons of previously existing state standards. A research-based approach is employed, assuring rigorous content and the application of higher-order skills (National Governors Association 2010).

Upon close reading, however, much of the math content is quite familiar. What's different, then? First, from a content perspective, it is the focus, coherence, and rigor of the current standards that differentiate them from earlier versions.

Today's Next Generation Tests (cont.)

What's Different about Today's Standards? (cont.)

Shifting Standards

Less is truly more! The focus of the standards significantly narrows the scope of the content, directing the time and energy of the math classroom toward deeper experiences on identified topics. But make no mistake, a focus on fewer standards is not a substitute for truly focused standards. These are not broad, general statements but specific, clear standards (National Governors Association 2010). This is a concerted effort to move away from the frequently cited "mile wide, inch deep" criticism first noted by Schmidt, McKnight, and Raizen in 1997. Today, there is less "coverage" to increase the depth of learning. In fact, "less topic coverage can be associated with higher scores on those topics covered because students have more time to master the content that is taught" (Ginsburg, A., 2005). The takeaway here is to teach less and learn more!

Serving as a vital link, coherent standards carefully connect learning within and across grades so students can build on understanding. Each standard is not a new event but an extension of previous learning.

Rigorous does not mean *harder*. Rather, this characteristic of the standards relates to application, skills, and conceptual understanding (Student Achievement Partners 2013). Conceptual understanding can be thought of as the ability to explain math to someone else, represent it in different ways, apply it to solve simple and complex problems, reverse givens and unknowns, and compare and contrast it to other concepts (Leinwand, Brahier, and Huinker 2014). This is a shift from thinking of math as a group of "tricks" to thinking of it as deep, connected understanding.

Even a cursory examination of the action verbs in the new standards reveals the need for conceptual understanding in addition to more skill-driven calculations and manipulations of numbers. A revealing exercise is to count the number of times verbs such as the following appear in the standards: *interpret, generate, understand, analyze, explain, relate, apply, extend, use,* and *evaluate.* Then, do a similar count of more skill-related verbs, such as *identify, write, graph, read, find, multiply, add, subtract,* and *divide.* Certainly, these skill-related verbs are still included and still significant. However, the higher-level thinking verbs figure more prominently.

Today's Next Generation Tests *(cont.)*

What's Different about Today's Standards? *(cont.)*

Standards–Driven Teaching

Another hallmark of today's standards is that math is more than content. There is now an emphasis on math processes such as reasoning, applying, connecting, and communicating (O'Connell and SanGiovanni 2013). The standards are not "new names for old ways of doing business" but a call to take next steps (National Governors Association, 2010). Teaching strategies used in classrooms should consistently include the processes of math as well as rich content.

"Mathematics is not nearly as much about speed and memorization as it is about being able to grapple with a novel problem, try various approaches from a collection of options, and finally reach an accurate answer" (Van de Walle, Karp, Lovin, and Bay-Williams 2014). We, as teachers, are learning techniques such as facilitating and questioning as we realize the importance of organization and careful task selection. We want our students to learn from one another through discussions in small and large groups. There are fewer skill-and-practice problems but more multistep problems. Vocabulary is emphasized and, above all, number sense, reasoning, and solving real problems are at the heart of our lessons (Van de Walle, Karp, Lovin, and Bay-Williams 2014).

Units of study are organized around strands of mathematics. These large groups of related standards serve as the big ideas that connect topics across grade levels. The strands are cross-cutting themes, serving as organizing principles for instruction. What unifies the strands? The processes of math and tasks that include higher-level thinking hold the strands together.

Our teaching and organization flow from the standards. The next inevitable step is our assessment, which is also is content- and process-driven.

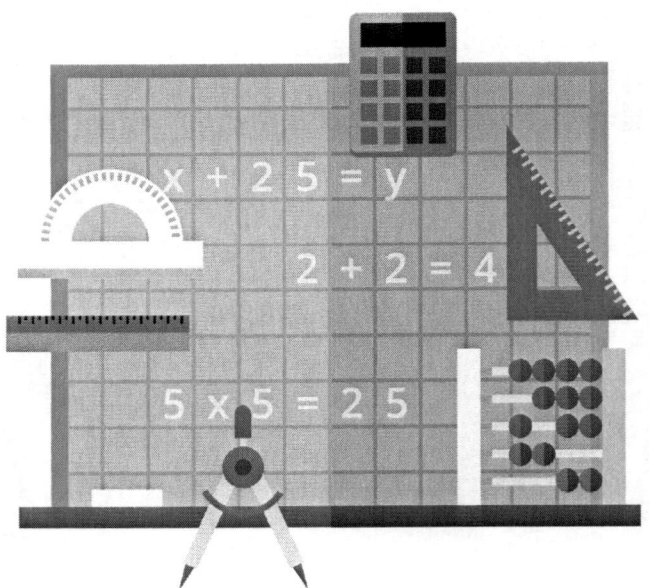

Today's Next Generation Tests *(cont.)*

What's Different about Today's Standards? *(cont.)*

This overview illustrates key mathematics concepts and thinking skills associated with each of the content strands. It deconstructs the critical understandings of the strands to identify the important "what" (concepts) and "how" (thinking skills) for teachers and students. Notice the repeated use of several higher-level thinking skills in many different content strands.

Strand	Key Concepts		Key Thinking Skills	
Operations and Algebraic Thinking	• addition • subtraction • multiplication • division • relationship between multiplication and division • multiplication and division facts within 100	• factors • multiples • numerical expressions • patterns • problems with the four operations	• analyze • explain • generate • identify • interpret • relate	• represent • solve • understand • use • write
Number and Operations in Base Ten	• place value system • multi-digit arithmetic	• properties of operations • decimals to hundredths	• generalize • perform	• understand • use
Number and Operations— Fractions	• unit fractions • fraction equivalence • fraction ordering • fraction comparison	• decimal notation for fractions • addition, subtraction, multiplication, and division of fractions	• apply • build • compare	• extend • understand • use
Measurement and Data	• time • liquid measures • volume • relationship of volume to multiplication and addition • masses of objects • conversion of measurements • data	• area • relationship of area to multiplication and addition • perimeter • linear vs. area measures • angle measures	• convert • distinguish • estimate • interpret • recognize	• relate • represent • solve • understand
Geometry	• shapes • attributes/properties • lines • angles • coordinate plane		• analyze • classify • compare • describe • draw	• graph • identify • reason • solve

(National Governors Association 2010; Van de Walle, Karp, Lovin, and Bay-Williams 2014)

Today's Next Generation Tests (cont.)

What's Unique about These Assessments?

Whether your summative assessment is specific to your state or from a multistate consortium, there are several unifying aspects of next generation assessments. The focus is on different question types that coincide with high-quality teaching of the standards. When analyzing the formats of the questions, descriptors such as *multistep questions, multi-answer multiple choice, higher-level questions*, and *complex-thinking questions* are frequently used. The emergence of piggyback questions, in which previous solutions are built upon for later solutions, is noted as well. Many of the tests are shifting to online platforms. All of this is in an effort to provide "evidence of proficiency with important mathematics content and practices" (Leinwand, Brahier, and Huinker 2014).

To gather this type of evidence, assessment prompts are structured to reveal understanding and reasoning. For example, examine these related problems:

"Traditional" Problem	Possible "Next Generation" Problem
8 + 12 =	Some friends went to the zoo. There were 8 girls. There were 12 boys. How many total friends went to the zoo?
Katie has 2 quarters, 3 dimes, and 9 pennies. How much money does she have?	Katie has 10 coins in her bank. She has more than $.50 but less than $1.50. What coins could she have? Prove that your solution is correct.
Find the area and perimeter of a 2 × 9 rectangle.	Draw two unique rectangles with areas of 18 square units. Are their perimeters the same or different? Why did this happen?
Jesse watches 2 hours of television every day. How many hours of television does he watch in one week?	Jesse watches 2 hours of television each day. How many hours does he watch in one year? How many hours will he watch in 10 years?
List the first 10 multiples of 5.	Do multiples of 5 always have a 5 in the ones place? Why or why not?
Solve 8 divided by $\frac{1}{4}$.	Write a story situation that shows 8 divided by $\frac{1}{4}$ and its solution.
Find the quotient and any remainder of 45 divided by 4.	Brandon has $45 on his coffee shop gift card. How many $4 iced coffees can he buy? Will he have any money left over? Prove your solution.

Today's Next Generation Tests *(cont.)*

What's Unique about These Assessments? *(cont.)*

The higher-level assessments are a response to the higher-level standards and teaching. As teachers move away from drill-and-kill rote memorization with its focus on getting quick, correct answers—or, in the words of math expert Phil Daro, "answer getting" (Ginsburg 2014)—and instead move toward a focus on thinking and using information for in-depth problems, the assessments also shift accordingly. These shifting exams include performance-based tasks rooted in problem-solving instead of some of the more traditional, standardized test questions of the past. A good way to think about it is instead of "teaching to the test," teachers today are "testing to the teaching." The more rigorous teaching is driving the assessments to be more rigorous as well.

Admittedly, the changing assessments and the one your state, district, or school ultimately chooses may still be in a condition of flux. However, regardless of the assessment or its final format, the emphasis on deep mathematical understanding and the students' abilities to communicate that understanding remains a central theme. Helping you to prepare your students for this level of understanding and communication is the goal of this resource.

What's Unique about This Resource?

Many test preparation guides are compilations of full-length practice tests. However, *TIME For Kids: Practicing for Today's Tests* is a collection of practice exercises. The focus is on higher-level mathematical thinking and the quality tasks that support it. Of course, strategies for effective test taking are reinforced. But these strategies are the strategies for mathematical thinking, higher-level teaching, and deep learning.

Partnering with TIME For Kids allows this resource the unique opportunity to use engaging images, math graphics, and real data for authentic, true math tasks. Such tasks are at the heart of standards-based teaching and assessing. Within the practice exercises, you will find the carefully constructed multiple-choice, multi-answer, and short-answer tasks students need to practice. Plus, practice exercises include TIME For Kids performance-based tasks to extend and enhance learning. There are significant opportunities for students to apply their learning and practice open-ended as well as structured problems under their teachers' guidance.

At its core, *TIME For Kids: Practicing for Today's Tests* is a collection of solid, standards-based mathematical tasks. It is the hope that these tasks will complement and support your teaching in the classroom.

In the words of one teacher, "It was not enough to teach better mathematics; I also had to teach mathematics better" (Rinehart 2000). If you find yourself coming to a similar realization, this resource is for you and your students!

Making It Meaningful

This section has been included to make this book's test practice more meaningful. The purpose of this section is to provide sample guiding questions framed around a specific practice exercise. This will serve as a meaningful and real-life application of test practice. Each guiding question focuses on strands of mathematics as well as test-taking strategies. The making-it-meaningful questions may be used with students as a teacher-led think aloud or to individually assess how students are approaching and understanding complex mathematical ideas and concepts. The framework used in this model serves as a template for how to approach all the practice exercises in this product. This template supports educators in preparing students for today's tests and helps make meaning of mathematical standards used in classrooms today.

When multiple choice questions have only one correct response, guide students in the following way:

"After reading the problem, can you use logical reasoning to eliminate any responses that do not make sense? How do you know they cannot be correct? Cross them out. Finally, reread and solve the problem, and select the best answer."

When problems include specific math vocabulary terms, help students in the following way:

"What math terms appear in the problem? Circle them. How can understanding the meanings of the terms help you solve the problem?"

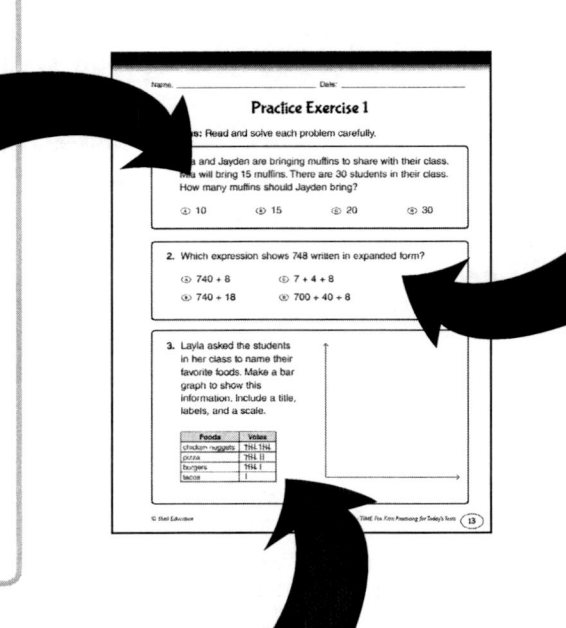

If students need to complete a table, chart, or graph, support them with the following guiding questions:

"What type of table, chart, or graph do you need to make? What information will it show? Do any components already appear? Which components do you need to add or include? Do you need to add any labels or titles to make your work complete and understandable to others?"

Making It Meaningful *(cont.)*

When a problem includes challenging numbers, provide support in the following way:

"Can you create a simpler but similar problem? How can solving the simpler problem give you any information about the actual solution?"

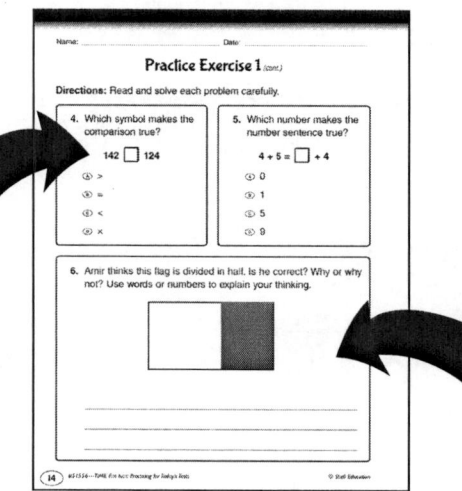

Math problems often include diagrams or models. Guide students in the following way to encourage active use of problem-solving strategies:

"What can you tell us about the diagram or model? Have you seen this, or something very similar, during previous learning? How can using what you already know help you solve the problem?"

When examining a table, chart, or graph, use guiding questions to help students organize their thinking and activate background knowledge:

"What type of table, chart, or graph is this? What questions can you answer based on the information given?"

When selecting an operation to solve a problem, prompt students:

"Reread the problem. What important words appear to help you choose the correct operation and make a plan to solve the problem? Should your answer be higher than the numbers in the problem? Should your answer be lower? Is there a way to check your calculations with an inverse operation?"

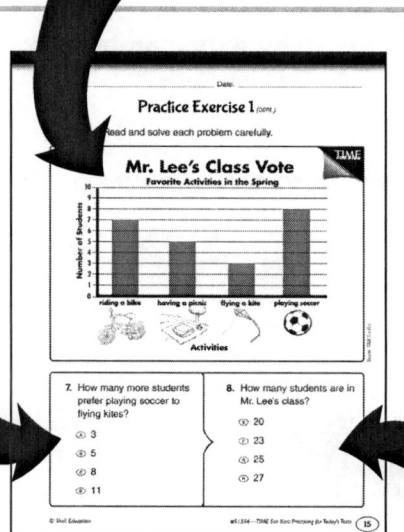

When solving problems with complex data, students should ask themselves:

"What information do I need to gather? Where can I find needed information? Is there any data given that I do not need to answer the question? How can I organize my thinking and data to make a plan and solve the problem?"

Making It Meaningful *(cont.)*

When students encounter questions asking for more than one answer, coach them to practice the following approach:

> "What are all the aspects of the problem? How is each answer unique from the others? How else can you approach the problem?"

For all open-ended problems, students should ask themselves the following questions:

> "Could I explain this problem to someone else? What am I being asked to do? Do I need to use my prior learning to solve this problem?"

For piggy-back problems that build on one another, direct students to:

> "Look at both problems. Underline all of the information from the first problem that can help you solve the second problem."

To support students in preparing for today's tests, send home the *Top Tips: Preparing for Today's Tests* on page 118. This page is intended to guide parents at home in how to prepare their children for tests. Page 119 gives students a list of strategies they can use at school to be more successful while taking tests.

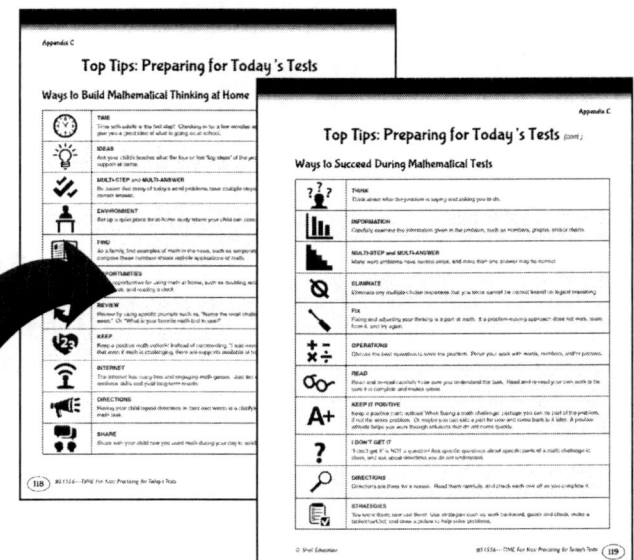

Practice Exercise 1

Directions: Read and solve each problem carefully.

1. Mia and Jayden are bringing muffins to share with their class. Mia will bring 15 muffins. There are 30 students in their class. How many muffins should Jayden bring?

   Ⓐ 10   Ⓑ 15   Ⓒ 20   Ⓓ 30

2. Which expression shows 748 written in expanded form?

   Ⓐ 740 + 8   Ⓒ 7 + 4 + 8

   Ⓑ 740 + 18   Ⓓ 700 + 40 + 8

3. Layla asked the students in her class to name their favorite foods. Make a bar graph to show this information. Include a title, labels, and a scale.

Foods	Votes
chicken nuggets	ⅢⅢ ⅢⅢ
pizza	ⅢⅢ II
burgers	ⅢⅢ I
tacos	I

Practice Exercise 1 *(cont.)*

Directions: Read and solve each problem carefully.

4. Which symbol makes the comparison true?

$$142 \;\boxed{}\; 124$$

(A) >

(B) =

(C) <

(D) ×

5. Which number makes the number sentence true?

$$4 + 5 = \boxed{} + 4$$

(A) 0

(B) 1

(C) 5

(D) 9

6. Amir thinks this flag is divided in half. Is he correct? Why or why not? Use words or numbers to explain your thinking.

_____

_____

_____

Practice Exercise 1 *(cont.)*

Directions: Read and solve each problem carefully.

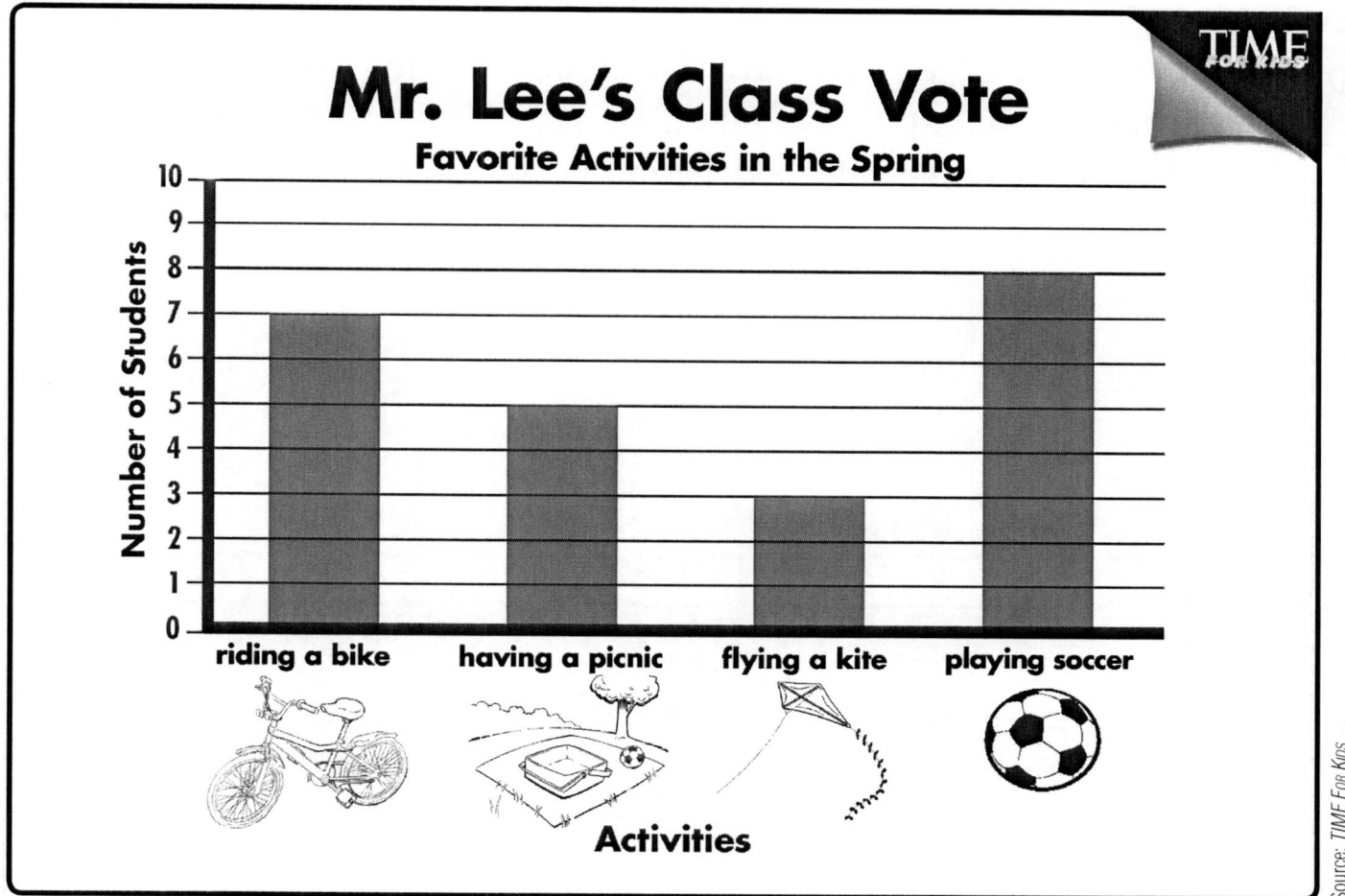

7. How many more students prefer playing soccer to flying kites?

- Ⓐ 3
- Ⓑ 5
- Ⓒ 8
- Ⓓ 11

8. How many students are in Mr. Lee's class?

- Ⓔ 20
- Ⓕ 23
- Ⓖ 25
- Ⓗ 27

Practice Exercise 1 *(cont.)*

Directions: Read and solve each problem carefully.

9. Next year, Mr. Lee will have 30 students in his class. He likes to group his students' desks in even rows. Draw **two** different ways Mr. Lee can set up the desks in his classroom.

10. Mr. Lee is planning the science experiment groups for next year. He wants students to work in groups of 3. How many groups should he have?

_____

11. Mr. Lee is planning some field trips for his class next year. He will need 6 chaperones for each trip. Mr. Lee will not have a group. How many students will be in each group?

_____

Practice Exercise 2

Directions: Read and solve each problem carefully.

1. Sophia is inviting 5 boys and 6 girls to her birthday party. How many party hats will she need to buy so that each guest gets a hat?

   Ⓐ 10

   Ⓑ 11

   Ⓒ 12

   Ⓓ 13

2. There are 4 party hats in each package. How many packages of party hats will Sophia need to buy?

   Ⓔ 1

   Ⓕ 2

   Ⓖ 3

   Ⓗ 4

3. Sophia and her dad are baking cupcakes for her party. They bake 4 rows of cupcakes. Each row has 3 cupcakes. Write a number sentence to show how many cupcakes Sophia and her dad will make.

   _____

Practice Exercise 2 *(cont.)*

Directions: Read and solve each problem carefully.

4. Which number will make this number sentence true?

$$84 - \boxed{} = 75$$

- Ⓐ 8
- Ⓑ 9
- Ⓒ 10
- Ⓓ 11

5. How many faces does this shape have?

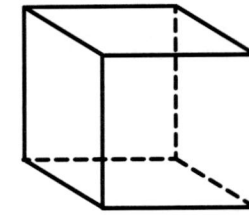

- Ⓐ 4
- Ⓑ 6
- Ⓒ 8
- Ⓓ 12

6. What time is shown on this clock?

_____

Practice Exercise 2 *(cont.)*

Directions: Read and solve each problem carefully.

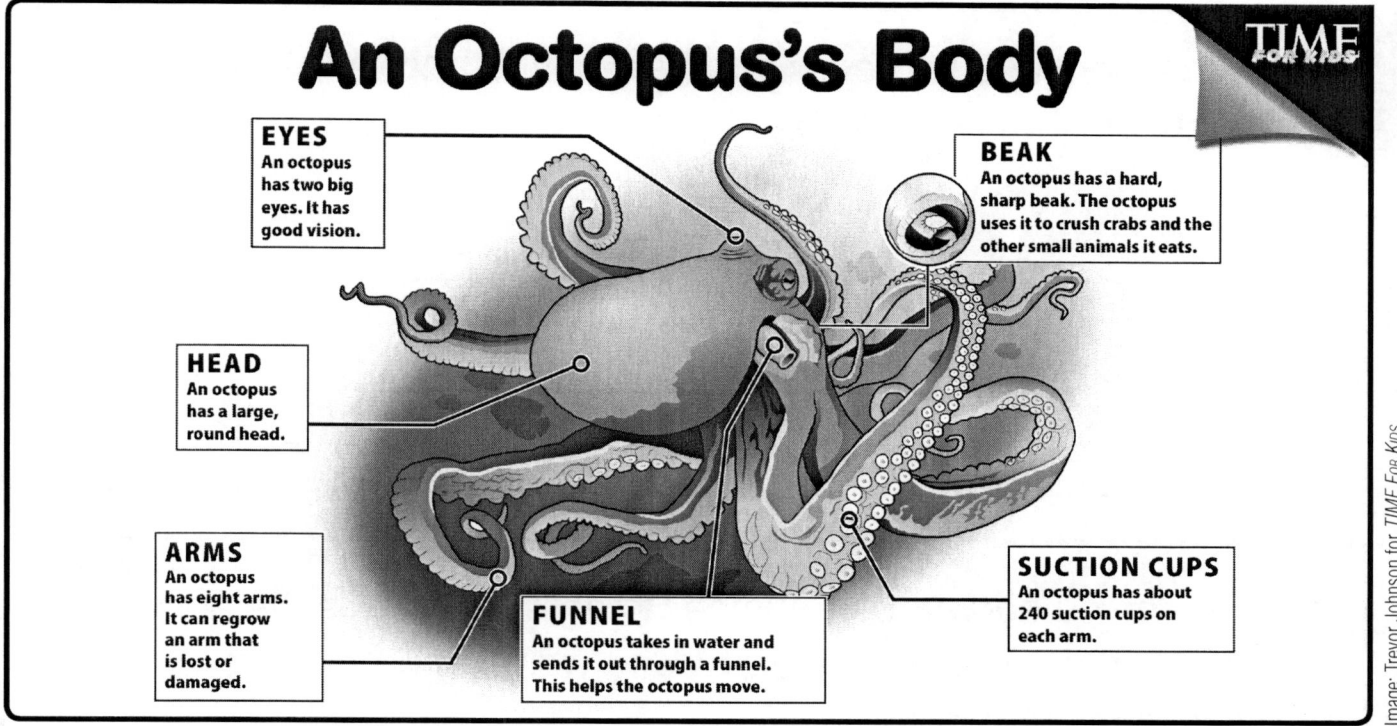

An Octopus's Body — TIME FOR KIDS

EYES
An octopus has two big eyes. It has good vision.

BEAK
An octopus has a hard, sharp beak. The octopus uses it to crush crabs and the other small animals it eats.

HEAD
An octopus has a large, round head.

ARMS
An octopus has eight arms. It can regrow an arm that is lost or damaged.

FUNNEL
An octopus takes in water and sends it out through a funnel. This helps the octopus move.

SUCTION CUPS
An octopus has about 240 suction cups on each arm.

Image: Trevor Johnson for *TIME FOR KIDS*

---

7. How many arms does an octopus have?

    Ⓐ 2   Ⓑ 4   Ⓒ 8   Ⓓ 24

---

8. Bianca and Amirah estimate the number of suction cups an octopus has on its whole body. Bianca says an octopus has no more than 1,600 suction cups. Amirah says Bianca's guess is too low. Which girl do you agree with, and why?

_____

_____

Practice Exercise 2 (cont.)

Directions: Read and solve each problem carefully.

9. When you add two even numbers, is the answer **always even** or **always odd**? Use words and numbers to explain your thinking.

   _____

   _____

   _____

10. When you add an odd number to an even one, is the answer **always even** or always **odd**? Use words and numbers to explain your thinking.

   _____

   _____

   _____

11. When you add two odd numbers, is the answer **always even** or **always odd**? Use words and numbers to explain your thinking.

   _____

   _____

   _____

Name: _____ Date: _____

Practice Exercise 3

Directions: Read and solve each problem carefully.

Isaiah is playing with this spinner. Use the spinner to complete the statements in problems 1–3.

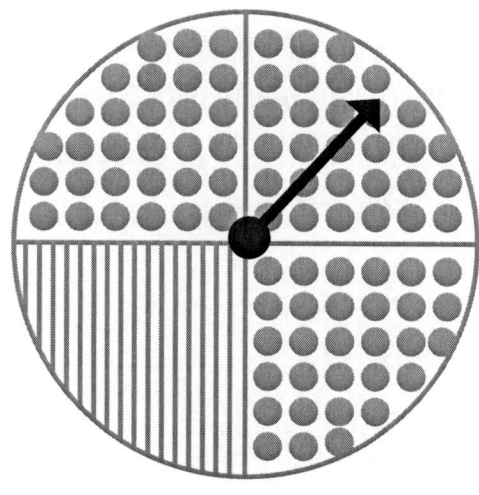

1. It is _____ that the arrow on the spinner will land on the dotted section.

- Ⓐ definite
- Ⓑ less likely
- Ⓒ impossible
- Ⓓ more likely

2. It is _____ that the arrow on the spinner will land on the striped section.

- Ⓔ definite
- Ⓕ less likely
- Ⓖ impossible
- Ⓗ more likely

3. What fraction of the spinner is **not** striped?

_____

Practice Exercise 3 *(cont.)*

Directions: Read and solve each problem carefully.

4. Which number makes the number sentence true?

$$100 - 65 = \boxed{}$$

- Ⓐ 25
- Ⓑ 30
- Ⓒ 35
- Ⓓ 165

5. Makayla has a box of 24 crayons. Brianna has a dozen more crayons than Makayla. How many crayons does Brianna have?

- Ⓐ 24
- Ⓑ 30
- Ⓒ 34
- Ⓓ 36

6. Draw **two** different shapes that have 4 sides and 4 right angles. Write the name of the shape under each shape.

_____   _____

Practice Exercise 3 (cont.)

Directions: Read and solve each problem carefully.

In a Chinese Zodiac Calendar, each year is named for an animal. To read the calendar, follow the years clockwise.

Image: *TIME FOR KIDS*

---

7. The year 2015 is the Year of the Sheep. Which year will be the next year of the Goat?

   ⓐ 2015   ⓒ 2025

   ⓑ 2016   ⓓ 2027

8. Which year will be the next Year of the Rat?

   ⓔ 2008   ⓖ 2018

   ⓕ 2010   ⓗ 2020

Practice Exercise 3 (cont.)

Directions: Read and solve each problem carefully.

June						
Sunday	**Monday**	**Tuesday**	**Wednesday**	**Thursday**	**Friday**	**Saturday**
	1	2	3	4	5	6
7	8	9	10	11	12	13
14	15	16	17	18	19	20
21	22	23	24	25	26	27
28	29	30				

9. Amelia is having a party on the third Saturday in June. What is the date of her party?

_____

10. What day of the week is 10 days after June 1?

_____

11. On which day of the week will July start?

_____

Practice Exercise 4

Directions: Read and solve each problem carefully.

1. Daniel has 35 pennies. He wants to trade his pennies for nickels. How many nickels will he get?

   (A) 3   (C) 7

   (B) 4   (D) 8

2. What is the value of the underlined digit?

   84_2_

   (A) 4   (C) 40

   (B) 14   (D) 400

3. Draw 3 rectangles. Under the first rectangle, write $\frac{1}{2}$. Under the second rectangle, write $\frac{1}{3}$. Under the third rectangle, write $\frac{1}{4}$. Divide and shade each rectangle to represent the fraction underneath it.

Practice Exercise 4 *(cont.)*

Directions: Read and solve each problem carefully.

4. Which **two** expressions have sums of 15?

    Ⓐ 8 + 8

    Ⓑ 8 + 7

    Ⓒ 9 + 5

    Ⓓ 10 + 5

5. Chloe has a total of 18 apples. Some of the apples are on the table. The other apples are in the basket. There are 9 apples on the table. How many apples are in the basket?

_____

6. Write 1,264 in expanded form.

_____

Name: _____ Date: _____

Practice Exercise 4 *(cont.)*

Directions: Read and solve each problem carefully.

How Much Sleep Do You Need?

Age	Recommended hours of sleep
Newborn 0–3 months	14–17 hours
Infant 4–11 months	12–15 hours
Toddler 1–2 years	11–14 hours
Preschool 3–5 years	10–13 hours
School age 6–13 years	9–11 hours
Teen 14–17 years	8–10 hours

Image: *TIME For Kids*

7. How much sleep is recommended for an eight-year-old?

   Ⓐ 9–11 hours

   Ⓑ 10–13 hours

   Ⓒ 11–14 hours

   Ⓓ 12–15 hours

8. What is the minimum amount of sleep recommended for a five-year-old?

   Ⓔ 8 hours

   Ⓕ 9 hours

   Ⓖ 10 hours

   Ⓗ 11 hours

Practice Exercise 4 (cont.)

Directions: Read and solve each problem carefully.

9.

Animal	Number of Animals	Total Legs

Tyler has lots of pets. He has 2 cats, 1 dog, 2 fish, and 3 birds. Create a chart to show the number of animals and the total number of legs for each type of animal.

10. Use the information from the chart above to draw a bar graph to show the total number of legs each type of animal has. Make sure to include a title, labels, and a scale.

Practice Exercise 5

Directions: Read and solve each problem carefully.

1. Anthony left school at 4:00 P.M. He played on the playground with his friend for 30 minutes. It took him 15 minutes to walk home. What time did he get home?

   Ⓐ 3:15 P.M.   Ⓒ 4:30 P.M.

   Ⓑ 3:30 P.M.   Ⓓ 4:45 P.M.

2. Which clock shows the time Anthony got home?

   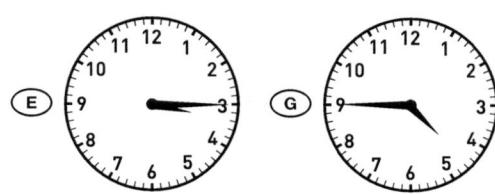

   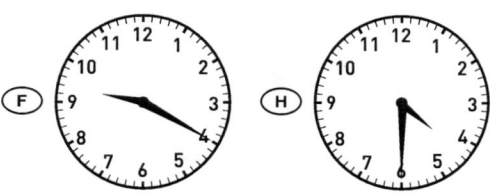

3. Use the centimeter ruler to measure each of the lines shown. What is the length of each line?

   ▬▬▬▬▬

   cm = _____

   ▬▬▬▬▬▬

   cm = _____

   ▬▬▬▬▬▬▬

   cm = _____

   ▬▬▬▬▬▬▬▬▬

   cm = _____

Practice Exercise 5 (cont.)

Directions: Read and solve each problem carefully.

4. Look at the pattern. Which numbers are missing?

   20, 25, 30, ____, 40, 45, ____

   - (A) 30, 40
   - (B) 35, 45
   - (C) 35, 50
   - (D) 40, 50

5. Which shape makes the base of this solid figure?

   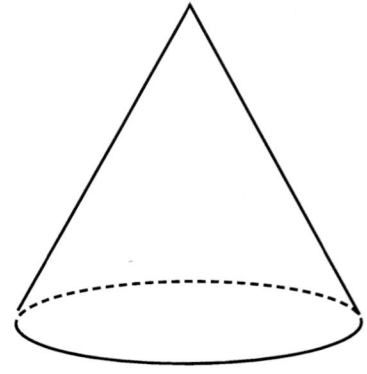

   - (A) cone
   - (B) circle
   - (C) square
   - (D) triangle

6. Tiffany swims 8 laps every Monday, Wednesday, and Friday. She swims 12 laps every Tuesday and Thursday. She does not swim on Saturday or Sunday. How many laps does Tiffany swim in one week?

   _____

Name: _____ Date: _____

Practice Exercise 5 *(cont.)*

Directions: Read and solve each problem carefully.

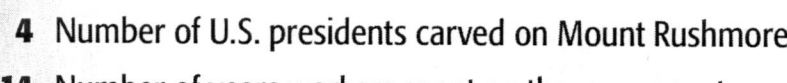

Mount Rushmore: By the Numbers

4 Number of U.S. presidents carved on Mount Rushmore

14 Number of years workers spent on the monument

20 Length, in feet, of George Washington's nose

60 Height, in feet, of each face

85 Weight, in pounds, of the drills workers used

400 Number of workers it took to build the monument

$1 MILLION About how much money the monument cost to build

Source: *TIME FOR KIDS*   Image: Courtesy of Karcher

---

7. About how many workers worked on each president's face?

Ⓐ 14

Ⓑ 85

Ⓒ 100

Ⓓ 400

8. If you stacked the presidents' faces, how high would the stack be?

Ⓔ 64 feet

Ⓕ 240 feet

Ⓖ 300 feet

Ⓗ 200 feet

Practice Exercise 5 *(cont.)*

Directions: Read and solve each problem carefully.

President	Height
Thomas Jefferson	189 cm
James Madison	163 cm
Abraham Lincoln	193 cm
Dwight D. Eisenhower	179 cm
John F. Kennedy	183 cm

9. How much taller was Lincoln than Kennedy?

_____

10. Create a **bar graph** to show the heights of the presidents. Make sure to include a title, labels, and a scale.

Practice Exercise 6

Directions: Read and solve each problem carefully.

1. How many corners does a rectangular prism have?

   Ⓐ 4

   Ⓑ 6

   Ⓒ 8

   Ⓓ 12

2. What is the value of the money shown?

   Ⓐ $1.43   Ⓒ $1.78

   Ⓑ $1.53   Ⓓ $1.88

3. Ryan had 23 toy cars. He got 13 toy cars for his birthday. He gave 6 toy cars to his little brother. Write a number sentence to show the number of toy cars Ryan has now.

   _____

Practice Exercise 6 *(cont.)*

Directions: Read and solve each problem carefully.

4. Which **two** answers show the value of the underlined digit?

   1,186

   - Ⓐ 8
   - Ⓑ 80
   - Ⓒ 8 tens
   - Ⓓ 8 ones

5. Which number makes the number sentence true?

   $$8 + \boxed{} = 16$$

   - Ⓐ 5
   - Ⓑ 8
   - Ⓒ 9
   - Ⓓ 10

6. Noah has 18 green balls. He counts the number of balls by 2. Write each number he will say.

   _____

   _____

   Noah's mom bought him more green balls. He now has double the green balls. Write a number sentence to show the number of the balls Noah has now.

   _____

Practice Exercise 6 *(cont.)*

Directions: Read and solve each problem carefully.

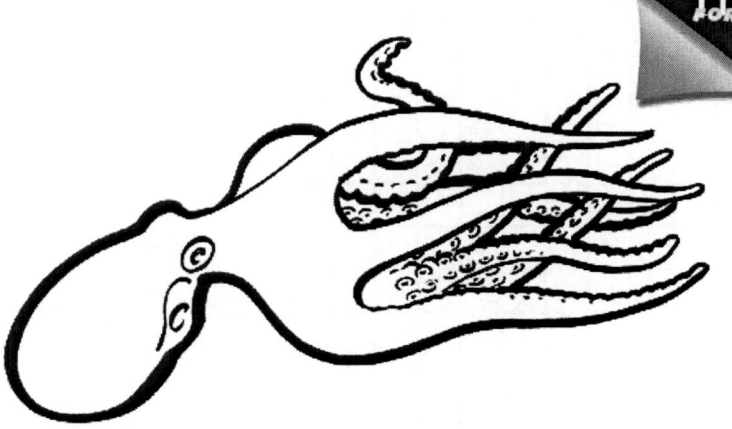

Octopus Facts

Giant Pacific Octopus	Common Octopus
Life span: 3 to 5 years	**Life span:** 1 to 2 years
Size: 10 to 16 feet	**Size:** 1 to 3 feet
Weight: 22 to 110 pounds	**Weight:** 7 to 22 pounds
What it eats: clams, fish, lobster, and shrimp	**What it eats:** crabs, crayfish, and mollusks

Source: *TIME FOR KIDS*

7. How much larger is the biggest giant Pacific octopus than the biggest common octopus?

Ⓐ 9 feet

Ⓑ 11 feet

Ⓒ 13 feet

Ⓓ 19 feet

8. How long can a giant Pacific octopus live?

Ⓔ 1–3 years

Ⓕ 2–4 years

Ⓖ 3–5 years

Ⓗ 5–8 years

Practice Exercise 6 *(cont.)*

Directions: Read and solve each problem carefully.

Aquarium A

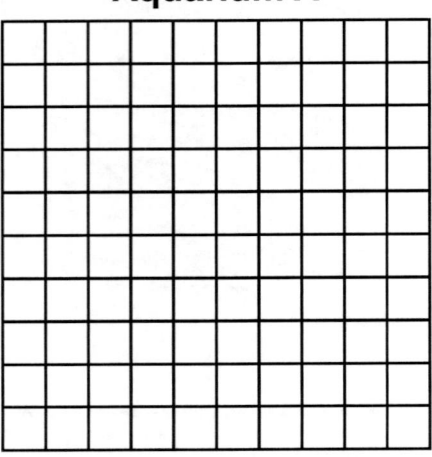

Aquarium B

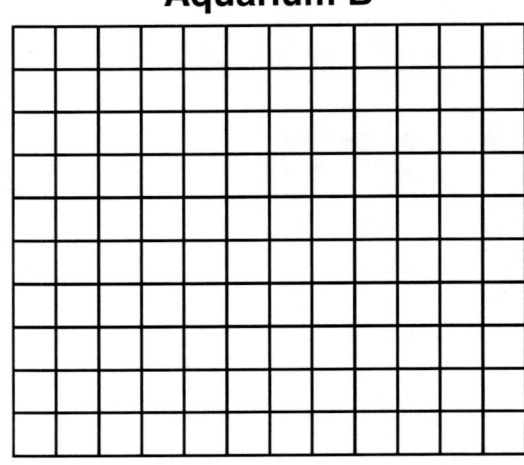

☐ = 10 square feet

9. Which aquarium will give the octopus more room to move? Use words and numbers to explain your answer.

_____

_____

10. Which aquarium has a shorter distance to walk around? Use words and numbers to explain your answer.

_____

_____

Practice Exercise 7

Directions: Read and solve each problem carefully.

1. What is the temperature on this thermometer?

   Ⓐ 60°F

   Ⓑ 62°F

   Ⓒ 67°F

   Ⓓ 65°F

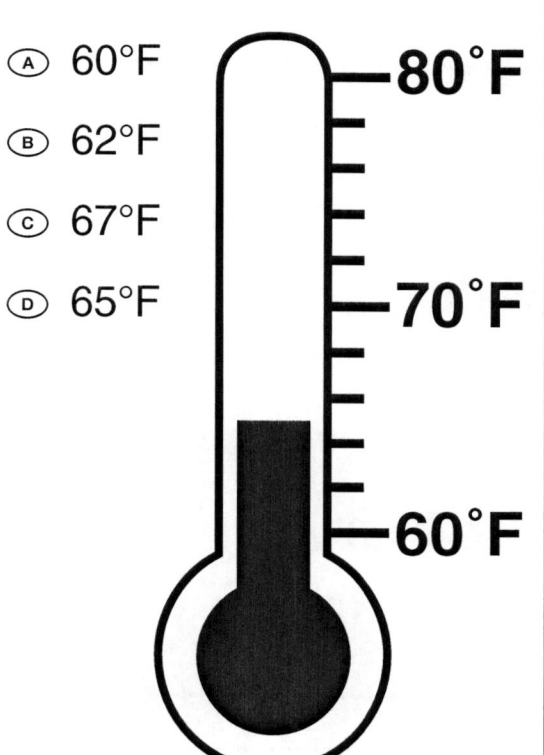

2. Which number makes the number sentence true?

$$38 + 24 = \square$$

   Ⓐ 52

   Ⓑ 62

   Ⓒ 71

   Ⓓ 82

3. Grace and Leah shared a watermelon. Grace ate $\frac{1}{4}$ of the watermelon. Leah ate $\frac{1}{8}$ of the watermelon. Who ate a bigger piece? Use words or numbers to explain your answer.

_____

_____

Name: _____   Date: _____

Practice Exercise 7 *(cont.)*

Directions: Read and solve each problem carefully.

---

4. Caleb has 11 trading cards. He wants to have 20. How many more cards does he need?

- Ⓐ 8
- Ⓑ 9
- Ⓒ 10
- Ⓓ 31

---

5. How many edges does a cube have?

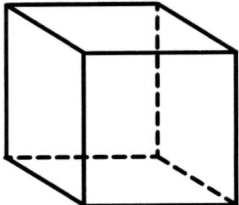

- Ⓐ 4
- Ⓑ 6
- Ⓒ 8
- Ⓓ 12

---

6. Show two different ways to solve 267 + 556.

Name: _____   Date: _____

Practice Exercise 7 *(cont.)*

Directions: Read and solve each problem carefully.

Mr. Garvey's Summer Survey

Would you rather go swimming or hiking?

Swimming	Hiking

Key: = one student

Source: *TIME FOR KIDS*

---

7. How many fewer students prefer hiking to swimming?

Ⓐ 3

Ⓑ 4

Ⓒ 5

Ⓓ 6

8. How many students are in Mr. Garvey's class?

Ⓔ 6

Ⓕ 11

Ⓖ 17

Ⓗ 20

Practice Exercise 7 *(cont.)*

Directions: Read and solve each problem carefully.

hot dogs . . . . pack of 10 for **$3.00**

hot dog buns . . . . pack of 8 for **$4.00**

box of one dozen cookies **$2.00**

box of 20 chip bags **$6.00**

juice boxes . . . . pack of 8 for **$2.00**

9. Mr. Garvey is planning a party for the 17 students in his class. He wants each student to have at least one of each item from the menu above. Complete the shopping list for Mr. Garvey so he can make sure to buy enough for the party.

Items	Cost	How many should he buy?	Total cost of item
hot dogs			
hot dog buns			
cookies			
chips			
juice boxes			

10. What is the total cost of all the items?

_____

Practice Exercise 8

Directions: Read and solve each problem carefully.

1. How many angles does this shape have?

   Ⓐ 4

   Ⓑ 5

   Ⓒ 6

   Ⓓ 10

2. Drake has 27 red marbles, 51 blue marbles, and 14 green marbles. About how many marbles does he have?

   Ⓐ 80

   Ⓑ 90

   Ⓒ 100

   Ⓓ 110

3. Draw 3 circles. Under the first circle write $\frac{1}{2}$, under the second one write $\frac{1}{3}$, and under the last one write $\frac{1}{4}$. Divide and shade each circle to represent the fraction under it.

Practice Exercise 8 *(cont.)*

Directions: Read and solve each problem carefully.

---

4. Which equation will help you solve $12 - 8 = \boxed{}$?

- Ⓐ $4 + 8 = 12$
- Ⓑ $6 + 6 = 12$
- Ⓒ $10 - 8 = 2$
- Ⓓ $12 + 4 = 16$

---

5. Justin has these coins in his pocket. How much money does he have?

- Ⓐ 43¢
- Ⓑ 58¢
- Ⓒ 98¢
- Ⓓ $1.03

---

6. Measure the line. What is the length of the line in inches? What is the length of the line in centimeters?

————————————

in. = _____

cm = _____

Why do you think the two measurements are different?

_____

#51556—TIME For Kids: Practicing for Today's Tests

Practice Exercise 8 (cont.)

Directions: Read and solve each problem carefully.

Three Sea Turtles

Animal	Kemp's ridley sea turtle	Leatherback sea turtle	Green sea turtle
Features	Greenish-gray shell with off-white or yellowish belly	Thick, rubbery shell that is flexible	Brown or green shell and a green body
Diet	Crabs, jellyfish, seaweed	Jellyfish	Mostly sea grass, algae
Size	Up to two feet long	Up to seven feet long	Up to five feet
Weight	Up to 100 pounds	Up to 2,000 pounds	Up to 700 pounds
Did you know?	The Kemp's ridley is the most endangered of all sea turtles.	The leatherback is the only sea turtle without a hard shell.	A green turtle's diet gives the animal's skin its green color.

Source: *TIME For Kids*

7. Which of these turtles grows to be the longest?

   Ⓐ giant sea turtle

   Ⓑ green sea turtle

   Ⓒ leatherback sea turtle

   Ⓓ Kemp's ridley sea turtle

8. If scientists found one of these sea turtles and it weighed 1,000 pounds, which type would it be?

   Ⓔ giant sea turtle

   Ⓕ green sea turtle

   Ⓖ leatherback sea turtle

   Ⓗ Kemp's ridley sea turtle

Practice Exercise 8 *(cont.)*

Directions: Read and solve each problem carefully.

Scientists studied 4 turtle nests. This chart shows the information from the study.

Nest	Number of Eggs	Meters from the Water
1	100	15
2	110	10
3	90	12
4	110	17

9. The hatchlings from which nest had to go the farthest to the ocean?

_____

10. Which nest had the fewest eggs?

_____

Practice Exercise 9

Directions: Read and solve each problem carefully.

1. Which **two** shapes show $\frac{1}{3}$ shaded.

   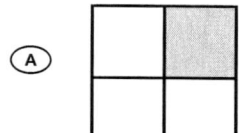

   Ⓐ

   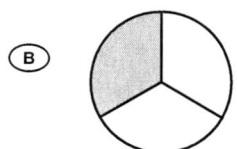

   Ⓑ

   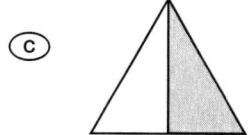

   Ⓒ

   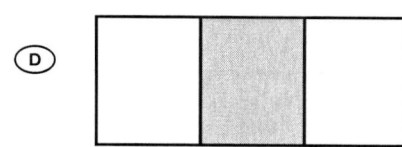

   Ⓓ

2. At his birthday party, William got 42 baseball cards from a friend. He got 19 baseball cards from another friend. He wanted to keep 40 baseball cards. He gave the other baseball cards to his little brother. How many baseball cards did he give his little brother?

   Ⓐ 11

   Ⓑ 21

   Ⓒ 37

   Ⓓ 40

3. Solve. Use words, numbers, or pictures to show your work.

   $$78 + 29 = \boxed{}$$

Practice Exercise 9 (cont.)

Directions: Read and solve each problem carefully.

4. Genesis buys some candy that costs 82¢. She gives the clerk $1.00. How much change does she get?

   Ⓐ 8¢

   Ⓑ 18¢

   Ⓒ 28¢

   Ⓓ $1.82

5. Select **three** expressions that equal 10.

   Ⓐ 5 + 5

   Ⓑ 6 + 4

   Ⓒ 7 + 2

   Ⓓ 9 + 1

6. Draw a shape that has 4 sides. Make two of the sides 2 inches long. Make the other two sides 1 inch long. What is the name of the shape you drew? What is the perimeter of the shape you drew?

   name = _____

   perimeter = _____

Name: _____ Date: _____

Practice Exercise 9 (cont.)

Directions: Read and solve each problem carefully.

 **Biggest Spiders**

① **Huntsman spider**
11.8 inches

② **Brazilian salmon-pink spider**
10.6 inches

③ **Brazilian giant tawny spider**
10.2 inches

④ **Goliath birdeater spider**
10 inches

⑤ **Wolf spider**
10 inches

Source: Scienceray.com   Image: Petra Wilfred

7. Which **two** spiders are the same size?

Ⓐ wolf spider

Ⓑ goliath birdeater spider

Ⓒ hunstman spider

Ⓓ Brazilian giant tawny spider

8. Which is the largest spider?

Ⓔ wolf spider

Ⓕ hunstman spider

Ⓖ goliath birdeater spider

Ⓗ Brazilian giant tawny spider

Name: _____ Date: _____

Practice Exercise 9 *(cont.)*

Directions: Read and solve each problem carefully.

9. Divide and shade each shape to show the fraction underneath it.

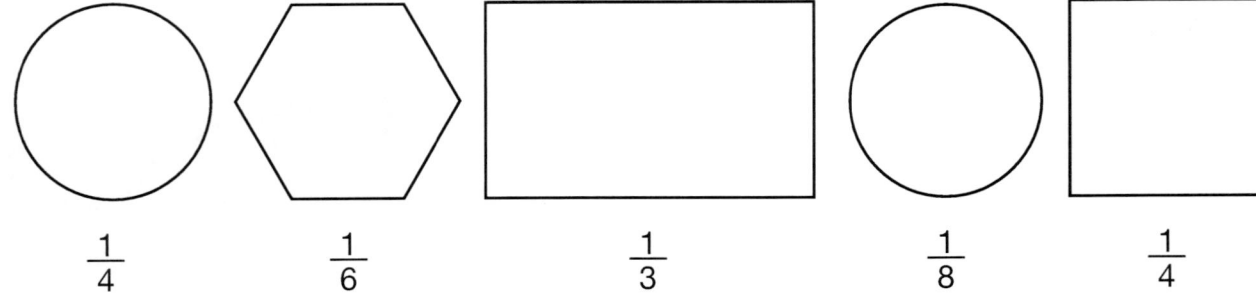

$\frac{1}{4}$ $\frac{1}{6}$ $\frac{1}{3}$ $\frac{1}{8}$ $\frac{1}{4}$

10. Which **circle** has the largest part shaded? Use words or numbers to explain your answer.

_____

_____

_____

_____

11. Is $\frac{1}{2}$ or $\frac{1}{3}$ larger? Use words or numbers to explain your answer.

_____

_____

_____

_____

Name: _____ Date: _____

Practice Exercise 10

Directions: Read and solve each problem carefully.

---

1. Which number makes the number sentence true?

$$85 + \boxed{} = 94$$

- Ⓐ 8
- Ⓑ 9
- Ⓒ 10
- Ⓓ 11

2. Kiara has a jump rope that is 60 inches long. Alexa has a jump rope that is 2 feet longer. How long, in inches, is Alexa's jump rope?

- Ⓐ 62
- Ⓑ 72
- Ⓒ 80
- Ⓓ 84

---

3. Seth had a total of 42 cherries. Some of the cherries fell out of the bowl onto the table. There are 8 cherries on the table. How many cherries are in the bowl? Write an equation to solve this problem.

_____

Practice Exercise 10 *(cont.)*

Directions: Read and solve each problem carefully.

---

4. Which **two** numbers would make this comparison true?

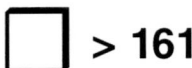 **> 161**

- Ⓐ 116
- Ⓑ 161
- Ⓒ 162
- Ⓓ 170

---

5. Which number is represented by the blocks shown?

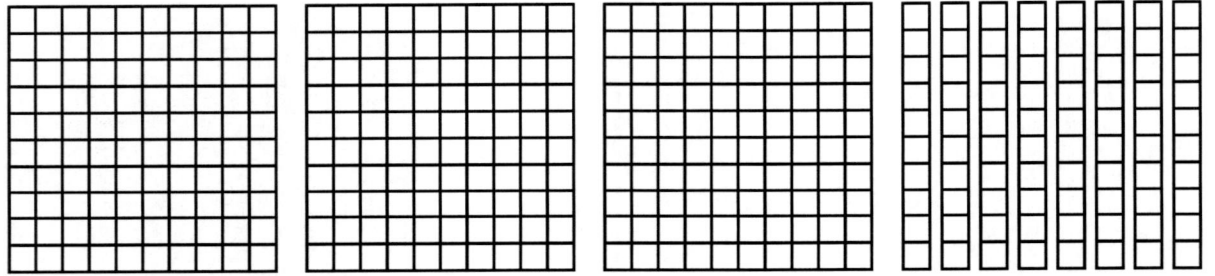

- Ⓐ 13
- Ⓑ 130
- Ⓒ 372
- Ⓓ 382

---

6. Draw two different shapes that each have a perimeter of 12 cm. Label the length of each side.

Name: _____ Date: _____

Practice Exercise 10 *(cont.)*

Directions: Read and solve each problem carefully.

Robot Producing Countries

① China 36,560 robots
② Japan 25,110
③ United States 23,700
④ South Korea 21,300
⑤ Germany 18,300

■ = 1,000 robots

7. Which country has the fewest robots?

   Ⓐ China

   Ⓑ Japan

   Ⓒ Germany

   Ⓓ United States

8. About how many more robots are in South Korea than Germany?

   Ⓔ 1,000

   Ⓕ 2,000

   Ⓖ 3,000

   Ⓗ 4,000

Name: _____ Date: _____

Practice Exercise 10 (cont.)

Directions: Read and solve each problem carefully.

9. Tim has a robot to help with chores. How many minutes will it take the robot to do all 5 chores?

Chore	Time to Complete (in minutes)
make bed	10
clean room	20
load dishwasher	15
take out the trash	15
mow the lawn	30

_____

10. How many minutes will it take the robot to make Tim's bed every day for a week?

_____

11. Tim has started mowing lawns for his neighbors. A charged robot can work for 2 hours. How many lawns can Tim's robot mow before needing to be recharged?

_____

Practice Exercise 11

Directions: Read and solve each problem carefully.

1. Which symbol makes this comparison true?

$$87 \; \square \; 88$$

- Ⓐ <
- Ⓑ >
- Ⓒ =
- Ⓓ ×

2. Which number completes this pattern?

670, 660, 650, 640, ____

- Ⓐ 620
- Ⓑ 630
- Ⓒ 650
- Ⓓ 680

3. Kayla is trying to read these two clocks. She says no time has passed between the two. Is she correct? Use words to explain your answer.

_____

_____

_____

Practice Exercise 11 *(cont.)*

Directions: Read and solve each problem carefully.

---

4. Lucas paints one face of a solid figure. When he presses the painted face on paper, it makes a square. Which **two** solid figures could he have?

   Ⓐ cube

   Ⓑ cone

   Ⓒ square pyramid

   Ⓓ triangular prism

---

5. Use the ruler to measure the lines shown. How many inches longer is Line B than Line A?

   Line A _____

   Line B _____

   Ⓐ 1   Ⓑ 2   Ⓒ 3   Ⓓ 8

---

6. Solve this equation using **two** different strategies. Use words, numbers, or pictures to show your work.

   $$135 - 68 = \boxed{}$$

Name: _____ Date: _____

Practice Exercise 11 *(cont.)*

Directions: Read and solve each problem carefully.

Dream Jobs

1 **Engineer** 621 responses

2 **Airplane or helicopter pilot** 565

3 **Doctor/nurse/EMT** 541

4 **Scientist** 500

5 **Teacher** 468

Source: LinkedIn   Image: Gary Lacoste for *TIME For Kids*

---

7. How many more people want to be scientists than teachers?

   Ⓐ 22

   Ⓑ 28

   Ⓒ 32

   Ⓓ 38

8. What is the most popular dream job?

   Ⓔ teacher

   Ⓕ engineer

   Ⓖ scientist

   Ⓗ airplane or helicopter pilot

Practice Exercise 11 (cont.)

Directions: Read and solve each problem carefully.

9. Mrs. Green asked her class to make a schedule for Career Day. Each of the 5 speakers will present for 15 minutes. How many total minutes will the speakers present?

_____

10. Each speaker will give a one-page handout to each student. How many sheets of paper will each student receive? Use words, numbers, or pictures to show your work.

_____

11. There are 25 students in Mrs. Green's class. How many handouts will the entire class get by the end of Career Day? Use words, numbers, or pictures to show your work.

_____

Name: _____ Date: _____

Practice Exercise 12

Directions: Read and solve each problem carefully.

1. Which symbol makes this comparison true?

 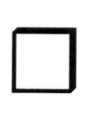 

  (A) >

  (B) <

  (C) =

  (D) $

---

2. Which number is missing from this pattern?

   3, 6, 9, 12, ____, 18, 21

   (A) 13

   (B) 14

   (C) 15

   (D) 17

---

3. Solve. Use words, numbers, or pictures to show your work.

   461 − 298 = ☐

   _____

Name: _____ Date: _____

Practice Exercise 12 *(cont.)*

Directions: Read and solve each problem carefully.

4. The perimeter of this rectangle is 24 centimeters. What is the length of each of the short sides?

8 cm

8 cm

Ⓐ 4 cm Ⓒ 16 cm

Ⓑ 8 cm Ⓓ 32 cm

5. Which number makes the number sentence true?

24 + ☐ = 100

Ⓐ 75

Ⓑ 76

Ⓒ 85

Ⓓ 86

6. How many faces are on this solid figure? _____

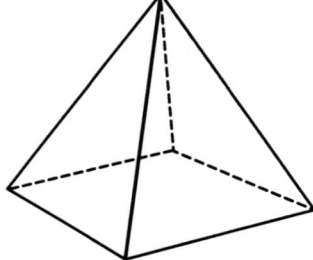

Are all of the faces the same shape? Use words or pictures to explain your thinking.

_____

#51556—TIME For Kids: Practicing for Today's Tests

Practice Exercise 12 (cont.)

Directions: Read and solve each problem carefully.

10,000 METER GOLD-MEDAL-WINNERS

8 medals **7** **3** Tie **2** **2**

  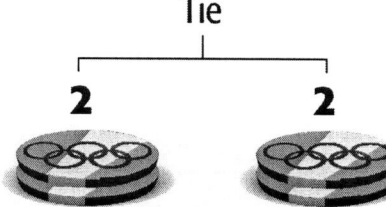

1 Ethiopia   **2** Finland   **3** U.S.S.R.*   **4** Czechoslovakia**   **4** Morocco

*The UUSR broke up into 15 countries, including Russia, in 1991.   **Czechoslovakia no longer exists.

Source: Olympic.org   Image: *TIME For Kids*

---

7. The runners from Ethiopia won 8 gold medals in the 10,000-meter race. How many total meters did they run to win all those gold medals?

Ⓐ 8,000

Ⓑ 10,000

Ⓒ 10,008

Ⓓ 80,000

8. How many more medals did Finland win than Morocco?

Ⓔ 5

Ⓕ 6

Ⓖ 8

Ⓗ 9

Practice Exercise 12 (cont.)

Directions: Read and solve each problem carefully.

9. Are both of these flags divided in thirds? How do you know?

_____

_____

10. Is this flag divided in thirds? How do you know?

_____

_____

 #51556—TIME For Kids: Practicing for Today's Tests

Practice Exercise 13

Directions: Read and solve each problem carefully.

1. Which number is represented by the blocks shown?

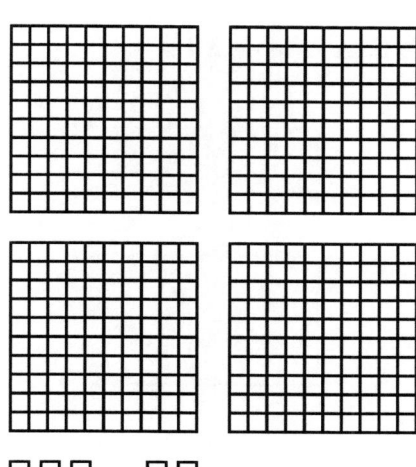 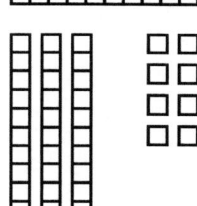 −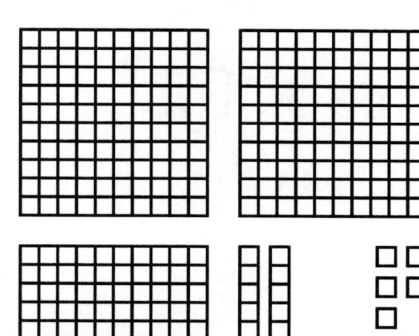

    Ⓐ 3   Ⓑ 25   Ⓒ 103   Ⓓ 113

2. Angela has 8 coins in her pocket. She has 87¢. She has 2 quarters, 3 dimes, 2 pennies, and one other coin. What is that coin?

    Ⓐ dime   Ⓒ nickel

    Ⓑ penny   Ⓓ quarter

3. Sean had 46 seashells in his bucket. When he got home, he only had 27 seashells. How many seashells fell out of his bucket?

_____

Practice Exercise 13 *(cont.)*

Directions: Read and solve each problem carefully.

4. Which number makes the number sentence true?

$$8 + 9 = \boxed{}$$

- Ⓐ 16
- Ⓑ 17
- Ⓒ 18
- Ⓓ 20

5. Which fraction represents the shaded portion of the shape?

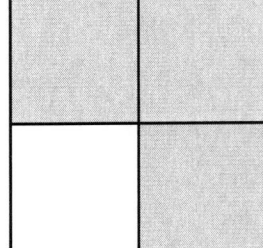

- Ⓐ $\frac{1}{4}$
- Ⓑ $\frac{1}{2}$
- Ⓒ $\frac{2}{3}$
- Ⓓ $\frac{3}{4}$

6. There are 742 students at Oak Elementary School. There are 383 boys. How many girls are at Oak Elementary School?

_____

Practice Exercise 13 (cont.)

Directions: Read and solve each problem carefully.

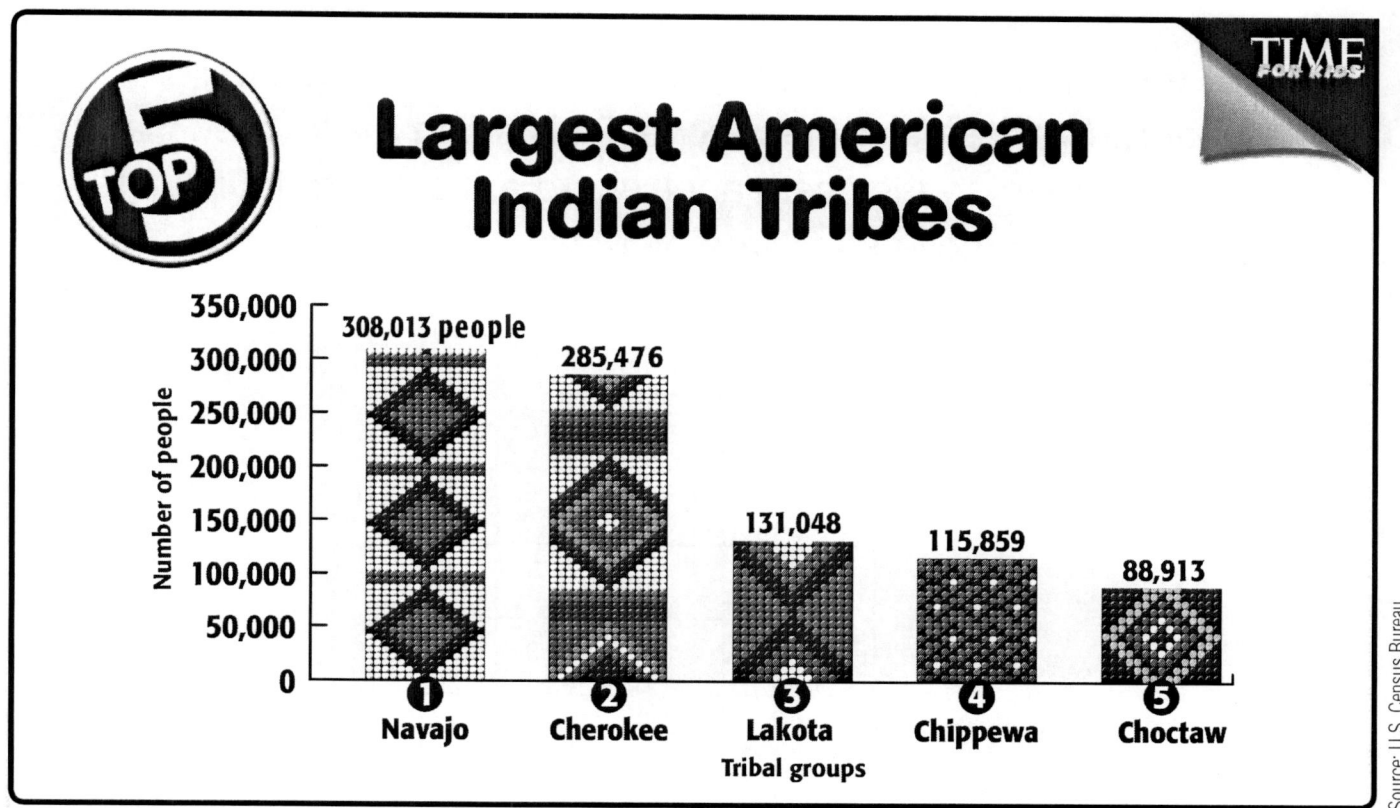

TOP 5

Largest American Indian Tribes

TIME FOR KIDS

Number of people

350,000
300,000 — 308,013 people
250,000
200,000 — 285,476
150,000 — 131,048
100,000 — 115,859
50,000 — 88,913
0

① Navajo ② Cherokee ③ Lakota ④ Chippewa ⑤ Choctaw

Tribal groups

Source: U.S. Census Bureau

---

7. Which tribe has the fewest members?

   Ⓐ Navajo

   Ⓑ Lakota

   Ⓒ Choctaw

   Ⓓ Cherokee

8. Which tribe has the most members?

   Ⓔ Lakota

   Ⓕ Navajo

   Ⓖ Cherokee

   Ⓗ Chippewa

Practice Exercise 13 *(cont.)*

Directions: Read and solve each problem carefully.

9. An early Choctaw settlement was discovered in Kemper County, Mississippi. When archeologists find a site, they make a grid pattern so they can label where artifacts are found. Draw a dig site that covers an area of 12 square feet.

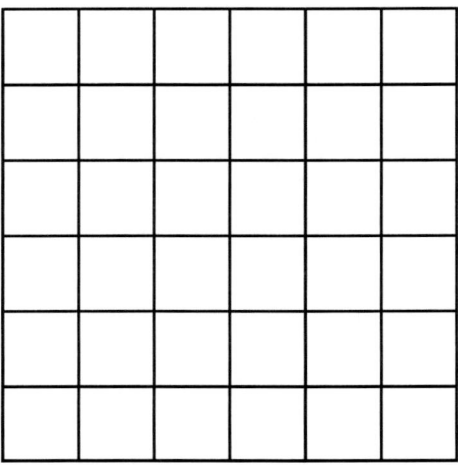

1 square cm = 1 square foot

10. What is the perimeter of the dig site you drew?

_____

11. If they doubled the size of the dig, would the perimeter change? How?

_____

_____

 #51556—TIME For Kids: Practicing for Today's Tests

Practice Exercise 14

Directions: Read and solve each problem carefully.

---

1. Which clock shows 3:30?

Ⓐ

Ⓑ

Ⓒ

Ⓓ

---

2. Complete the pattern.

900, 800, 700, ____, 500, 400, ____

ⓐ 600, 200   ⓑ 600, 300   ⓒ 800, 200   ⓓ 800, 300

---

3. Draw **three** different shapes that have 4 sides each.

Practice Exercise 14 *(cont.)*

Directions: Read and solve each problem carefully.

4. The students in Mrs. Brown's class sit in groups. There are 6 groups. There are 4 students in each group. How many students are in Mrs. Brown's class?

Ⓐ 10

Ⓑ 20

Ⓒ 23

Ⓓ 24

5. Which symbol makes the comparison true?

896 ☐ 868

Ⓐ <

Ⓑ >

Ⓒ =

Ⓓ ×

6. Grace has 11 nickels in her piggy bank. How much money does she have? _____

Explain how she would count her nickels to know how much money she has.

_____

_____

Grace is saving to buy a puzzle that costs $2.00. How many more nickels does she need?

_____

Practice Exercise 14 *(cont.)*

Directions: Read and solve each problem carefully.

TOP 5 Issues for the President

1,000 kids voted on the most important issues facing Barack Obama.

1 **The economy**
454 kids

2 **Keeping the country safe**
111 kids

3 **The environment**
106 kids

4 **Health care**
103 kids

5 **Education**
88 kids

Sources: *TIME For Kids* and Kidshealth.org poll   Image: Shutterstock.com and Filip Fuxa

7. What is the most important issue for the president?

ⓐ crime

ⓑ economy

ⓒ education

ⓓ environment

8. How many more kids want the president to focus on keeping the country safe than on education?

ⓔ 23

ⓕ 113

ⓖ 114

ⓗ 117

Practice Exercise 14 *(cont.)*

Directions: Read and solve each problem carefully.

9. Sara completes chores to raise money for a new video game. This chart shows how much she earns for each task. She has time to do one chore a day. She rakes leaves on Monday and Friday. She washes cars on Tuesday and Wednesday. She mows lawns on Saturday and Sunday, and she takes out the trash Thursday. How much money does Sara make in a week?

Chore	Amount Earned
rake leaves	$2
wash car	$3
mow lawn	$4
take out the trash	$1

_____

10. Create a bar graph to show the money earned from each chore.

Practice Exercise 15

Directions: Read and solve each problem carefully.

1. Which number makes the number sentence true?

$$88 + \boxed{} = 100$$

- Ⓐ 12
- Ⓑ 13
- Ⓒ 22
- Ⓓ 23

2. Which **two** expressions have values equal to 13?

- Ⓐ 5 + 5
- Ⓑ 6 + 7
- Ⓒ 9 + 4
- Ⓓ 10 + 1

3. Christopher's school had a jump rope fundraiser. The students raised pledges of $2.00 per jump. How much money did the students raise for the school?

Grade	Number of Jumps
K	200
1	120
2	230
3	250
4	140
5	110

_____

Practice Exercise 15 *(cont.)*

Directions: Read and solve each problem carefully.

4. Which **two** sets of circles have $\frac{3}{4}$ of the circles shaded?

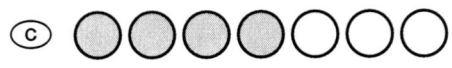

5. How many centimeters larger is the perimeter of Square B than the perimeter of Square A?

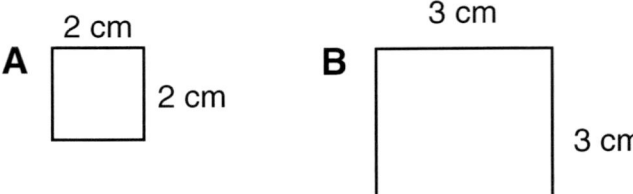

Ⓐ 1   Ⓑ 2   Ⓒ 3   Ⓓ 4

6. Kay's schedule is partially filled in.

Help her fill in the missing spaces using these clues.

Event	Time
language arts	9:00
lunch	11:00
math	
recess	
science	1:30
art	2:15
dismissal	3:00

- Lunch is 30 minutes. What time does math start? _____

- Math is 90 minutes. What time does recess start?

  _____

- How long is recess? _____

Practice Exercise 15 (cont.)

Directions: Read and solve each problem carefully.

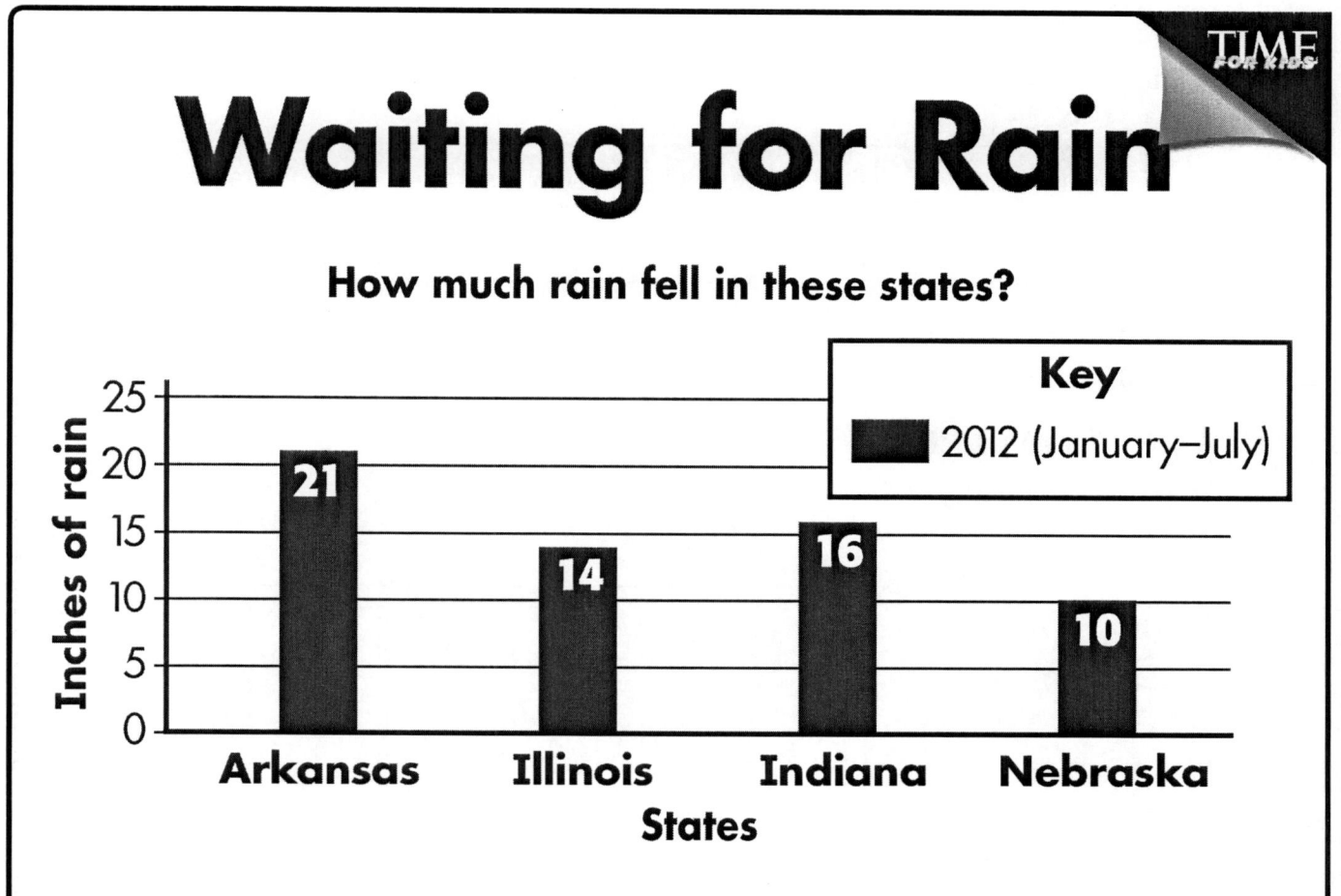

Waiting for Rain

How much rain fell in these states?

Key: 2012 (January–July)

Inches of rain / States

Arkansas 21, Illinois 14, Indiana 16, Nebraska 10

Source: National Oceanic and Atmospheric Administration

7. From January to July in 2012, which state had the least amount of rain?

Ⓐ Illinois

Ⓑ Indiana

Ⓒ Nebraska

Ⓓ Arkansas

8. Which state had an odd number of inches of rain?

Ⓔ Illinois

Ⓕ Indiana

Ⓖ Nebraska

Ⓗ Arkansas

Practice Exercise 15 (cont.)

Directions: Read and solve each problem carefully.

Eli recorded the weather in New York City for 8 days.

Day 1 – sunny	Day 3 – sunny	Day 5 – sunny	Day 7 – raining
Day 2 – raining	Day 4 – cloudy	Day 6 – sunny	Day 8 – cloudy

9. Use the information in the chart to create a bar graph. Make sure to include a title, labels, and a scale.

10. How many more days were sunny than cloudy?

_____

11. What fraction of the days did it rain?

_____

Name: _____ Date: _____

Practice Exercise 16

Directions: Read and solve each problem carefully.

1. Which equation could you use to check the problem shown?

$$64 + 36 = 100$$

Ⓐ $60 - 30 = 30$

Ⓑ $64 - 36 = 28$

Ⓒ $100 - 64 = 36$

Ⓓ $100 + 36 = 136$

2. Which number makes the number sentence true?

$$94 - 16 = \boxed{}$$

Ⓐ 70

Ⓑ 78

Ⓒ 80

Ⓓ 82

3. Circle all the shapes that have $\frac{1}{2}$ shaded. Then, draw a shape of your own that has $\frac{1}{2}$ shaded.

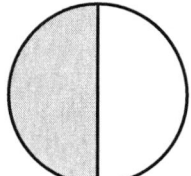  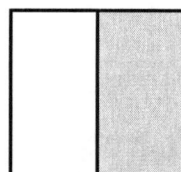 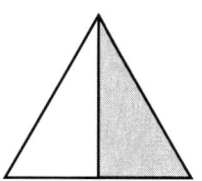 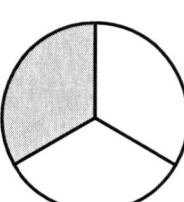

Practice Exercise 16 *(cont.)*

Directions: Read and solve each problem carefully.

---

4. What is the value of the money shown?

(A) $1.27   (C) $1.62

(B) $1.50   (D) $1.67

---

5. Tristan saw 12 geese on the pond. Some flew away. There are 5 geese left. How many geese flew away?

(A) 5   (C) 7

(B) 6   (D) 12

---

6. Describe this pattern.

100, 90, 80, 70, 60, 50

_____

_____

_____

Name: _____   Date: _____

Practice Exercise 16 (cont.)

Directions: Read and solve each problem carefully.

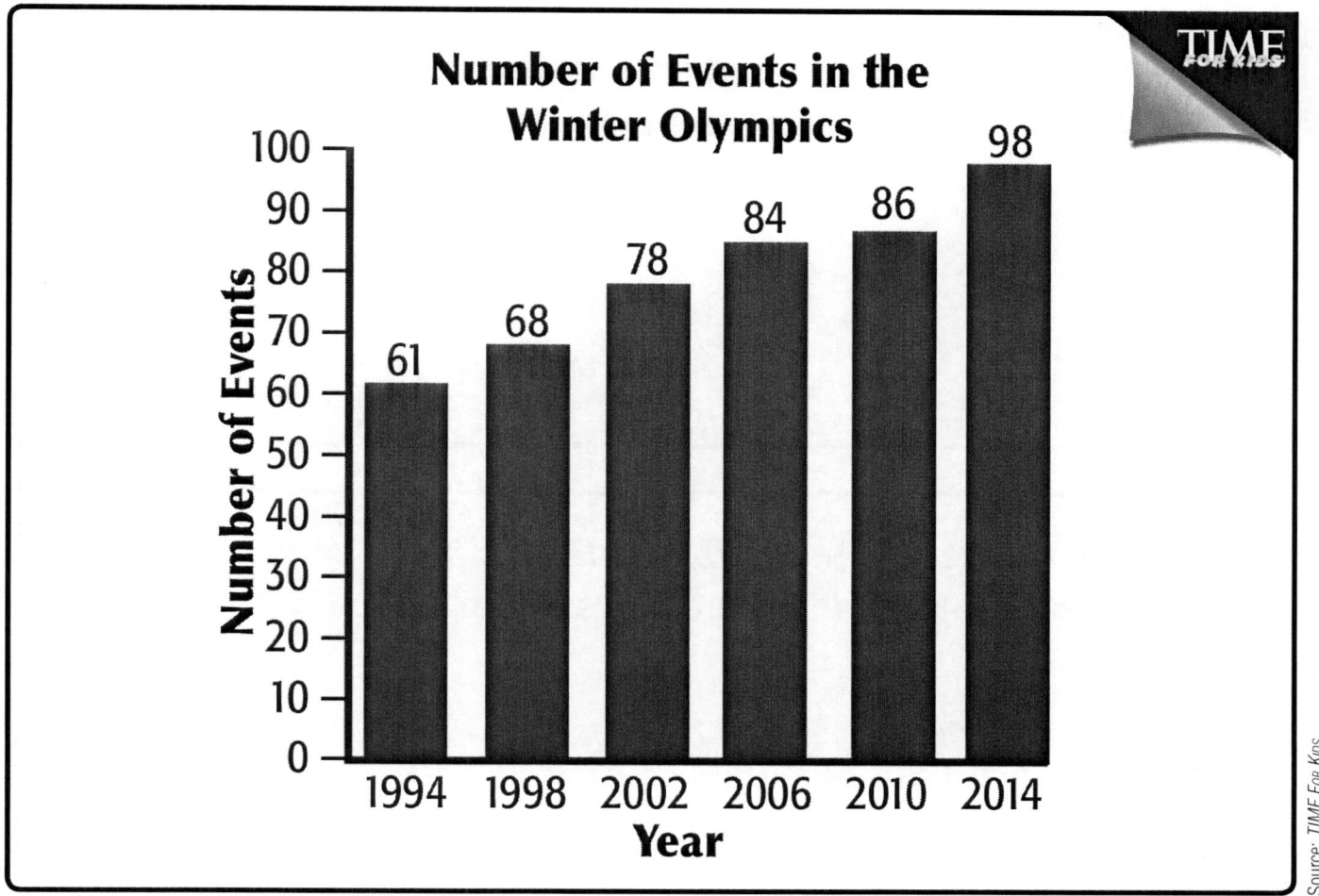

Number of Events in the Winter Olympics

7. How many events were added from 1994 to 2010?

   Ⓐ 17

   Ⓑ 23

   Ⓒ 25

   Ⓓ 37

8. Between which years were the fewest number of events added?

   Ⓔ 1994–1998

   Ⓕ 2002–2006

   Ⓖ 2006–2010

   Ⓗ 2010–2014

Practice Exercise 16 (cont.)

Directions: Read and solve each problem carefully.

9. Based on the graph, *Number of Events in the Winter Olympics*, how many more events were played in 2014 than in 1994?

_____

10. Based on the graph, *Number of Events in the Winter Olympics*, how many total events were played from 1994 to 2014?

_____

11. There will be 102 events in the 2018 Winter Olympics. Each event will award a gold, a silver, and a bronze medal to the winners. How many medals will be given in 2018?

_____

Name: _____ Date: _____

Practice Exercise 17

Directions: Read and solve each problem carefully.

1. Which number makes the number sentence true?

   $24 + 46 + 12 + 15 = \square$

   (A) 77   (C) 97

   (B) 87   (D) 107

2. Which number makes the number sentence true?

   $9 + 9 = \square$

   (A) 16   (C) 19

   (B) 18   (D) 20

3. Use the picture graph to answer the questions.

| | | = 2 cups of lemonade sold |

Monday   Tuesday   Wednesday   Thursday   Friday

Write an equation to show how many cups of lemonade were sold in total on Monday, Tuesday, Wednesday, and Thursday.

_____

There were a total of 30 cups of lemonade sold from Monday to Friday. How many cups were sold on Friday?

_____

Practice Exercise 17 *(cont.)*

Directions: Read and solve each problem carefully.

---

4. How many faces are there on all of these blocks?

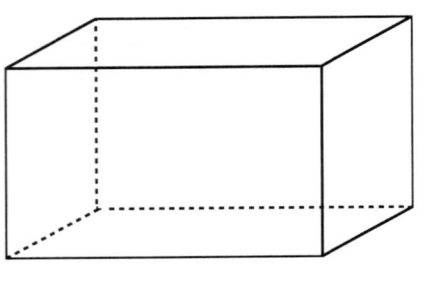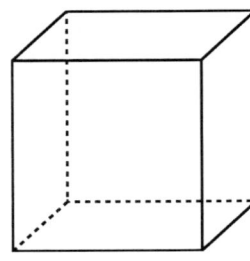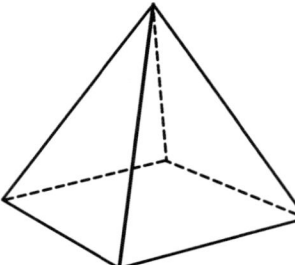

    Ⓐ 12   Ⓑ 13   Ⓒ 17   Ⓓ 18

---

5. What would be the most appropriate tool to use to measure the width, in inches, of a bulletin board in your classroom?

    Ⓐ ruler   Ⓒ meter stick

    Ⓑ yardstick   Ⓓ centimeter cubes

---

6. This clock shows 4:15. Another way to say this time is "a quarter after 4." Explain why.

_____

_____

_____

_____

Practice Exercise 17 (cont.)

Directions: Read and solve each problem carefully.

A gym teacher is planning Field Day. Here is a schedule of the events for grades K–2.

Field Day Schedule			
Event	**Start time**	**End time**	**Number of volunteers needed**
Egg Race	12:15	12:30	3
Football Toss	12:30	12:45	3
Tug Of War	12:45	1:00	4
Scooter Race	1:00	1:15	4
Half-Mile Race	1:15	1:30	4
Water Break	1:30	1:45	3
Batting Practice	1:45	2:00	3
Parachute Play	2:00	2:15	4

7. Ms. Wright has 24 students. She needs to make equal groups for each event. How many students will go to each event at one time?

Ⓐ 3

Ⓑ 4

Ⓒ 10

Ⓓ 12

8. How many volunteers are needed for Field Day?

Ⓔ 20

Ⓕ 24

Ⓖ 27

Ⓗ 28

Practice Exercise 17 *(cont.)*

Directions: Read and solve each problem carefully.

9. Based on the chart on page 79, how many minutes will the Field Day events last?

    _____

10. How long will it take the students to complete the first 5 events on Field Day?

    _____

    _____

    _____

11. The students ate snack for 30 minutes after the last event. How long did the entire Field Day last?

    _____

Name: _____   Date: _____

Practice Exercise 18

Directions: Read and solve each problem carefully.

1. What time does this clock show?

   Ⓐ 4:30

   Ⓑ 4:45

   Ⓒ 5:30

   Ⓓ 5:45

2. Look at the clock shown above. What time will it be in 15 minutes?

   Ⓔ 4:00

   Ⓕ 4:30

   Ⓖ 5:00

   Ⓗ 6:00

3. Solve and check your answer.

   862 – 475 = ⬚

   _____

Practice Exercise 18 (cont.)

Directions: Read and solve each problem carefully.

4. Which number makes the number sentence true?

$$14 - \boxed{} = 7$$

- (A) 6
- (B) 7
- (C) 8
- (D) 9

5. Wayne drew a shape with 2 long sides, 2 short sides, and 4 right angles. What shape did he draw?

- (A) square
- (B) rhombus
- (C) trapezoid
- (D) rectangle

6. Write **six** different addition number sentences that have a value of 10.

Practice Exercise 18 (cont.)

Directions: Read and solve each problem carefully.

7. Alexis made this chart to show the top meals voted by the students in her school. She forgot to label the sections with the food choices. Add the correct labels to the chart using this information.

- Half of the students chose pizza as their favorite meal.

- The least amounts of votes went to peanut butter and jelly sandwiches.

- The same number of students selected hamburgers and burritos as their favorite meals.

- $\frac{1}{4}$ of the students preferred the salad bar.

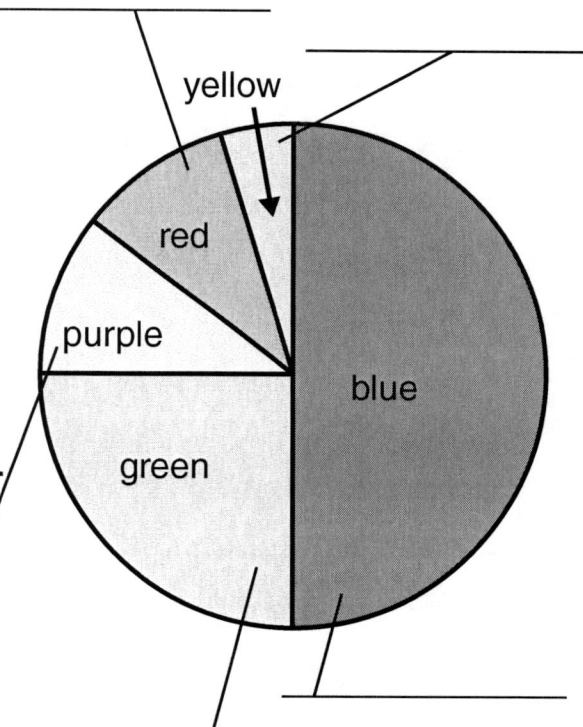

8. There were 100 students surveyed. How many students chose hamburgers and burritos combined?

    Ⓐ 10   Ⓑ 20   Ⓒ 30   Ⓓ 40

Name: _____   Date: _____

Practice Exercise 18 *(cont.)*

Directions: Read and solve each problem carefully.

1 mango equals 5 servings

1 box = 10 mangoes

---

9. How many students can be served with 10 mangoes?

_____

---

10. How many boxes are needed to hold 130 mangoes?

_____

11. Each box of mangoes costs $8.00. How many mangoes can be purchased with $24.00?

_____

#51556—TIME FOR KIDS: Practicing for Today's Tests

Name: _____ Date: _____

Practice Exercise 19

Directions: Read and solve each problem carefully.

1. Which place value combination completes this problem?

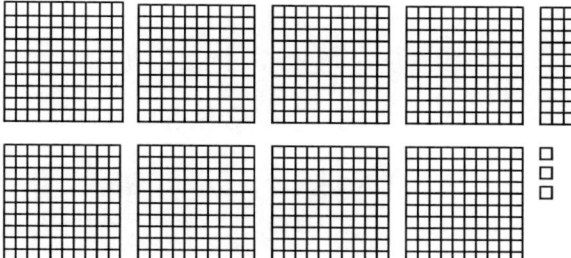 −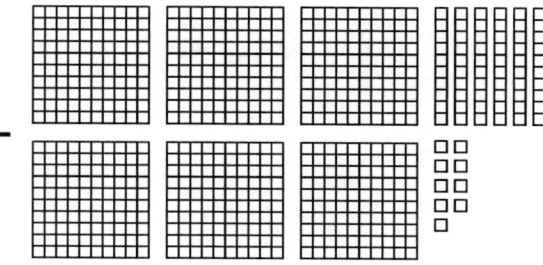

Ⓐ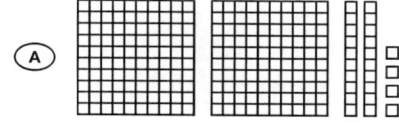

Ⓒ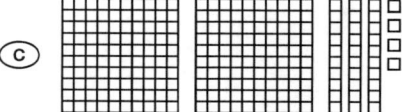

Ⓑ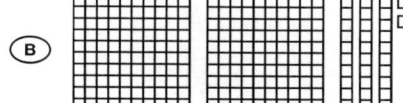

Ⓓ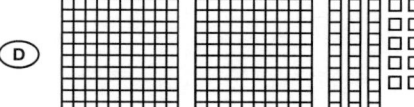

---

2. Identify the shape shown.

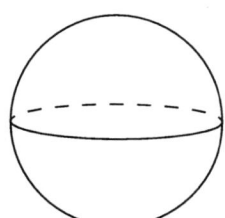

Ⓐ cone   Ⓒ sphere

Ⓑ circle   Ⓓ cylinder

---

3. What symbol would complete this comparison?

23 ☐ 33

Practice Exercise 19 (cont.)

Directions: Read and solve each problem carefully.

4. Which number makes the number sentence true?

$$4 + 3 + 7 + 10 = \boxed{}$$

Ⓐ 14

Ⓑ 22

Ⓒ 24

Ⓓ 34

5. A movie started at the time shown on Clock A. The movie ended at the time shown on Clock B. How long was the movie?

Clock A   **Clock B**

Ⓐ 1 hour

Ⓑ 2 hours

Ⓒ 30 minutes

Ⓓ 1 hour and 30 minutes

6. Write an equation to represent the picture shown. Solve the equation.

_____

Practice Exercise 19 (cont.)

Directions: Read and solve each problem carefully.

cup	pint	quart	gallon
cup			
cup	pint		
cup			
cup	pint	quart	
cup			
cup	pint		
cup			
cup	pint	quart	
cup			
cup	pint		
cup			
cup	pint	quart	
cup			
cup	pint		
cup			

7. How many cups are in one quart?

   (A) 1

   (B) 2

   (C) 4

   (D) 8

8. How many one-cup containers would a gallon of water fill?

   (E) 4

   (F) 8

   (G) 12

   (H) 16

Name: _____ Date: _____

Practice Exercise 19 (cont.)

Directions: Read and solve each problem carefully.

Here is the recipe for making one quart of fruit punch:

- 1 pint of apple juice
- 1 cup of orange juice
- 1 cup of ginger ale

9. Rafael needs to triple this recipe to make 3 quarts of punch for a party. Write the new fruit punch recipe in the box provided.

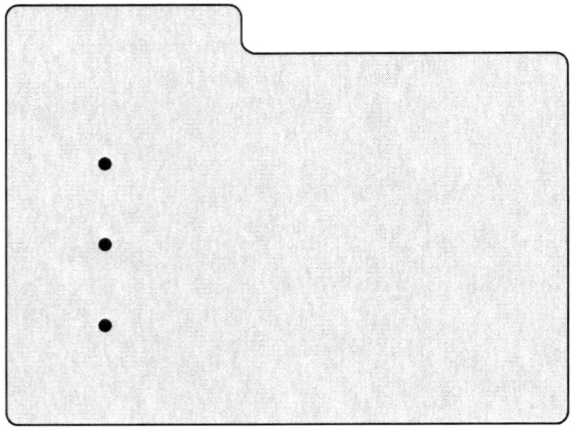

-
-
-

10. How many cups of apple juice and orange juice does Rafael need to make the new recipe?

_____

#51556—*TIME For Kids: Practicing for Today's Tests* © *Shell Education*

Name: _____   Date: _____

Practice Exercise 20

Directions: Read and solve each problem carefully.

1. Rebecca, Diego, and Kevin are making cards for their friends. Rebecca makes 8 cards. Diego makes 7 cards. Kevin makes the same number of cards as Rebecca. How many cards did they make for their friends?

   Ⓐ 7

   Ⓑ 8

   Ⓒ 15

   Ⓓ 16

2. What is the value of the coins shown?

   Ⓐ 57¢   Ⓒ $1.05

   Ⓑ 97¢   Ⓓ $1.17

3. Zion's mother cut an apple into 12 pieces. Zion wants to share his apple with 5 friends. How can Zion and his friends share the apple equally?

Name: _____ Date: _____

Practice Exercise 20 *(cont.)*

Directions: Read and solve each problem carefully.

4. What is the perimeter of this shape?

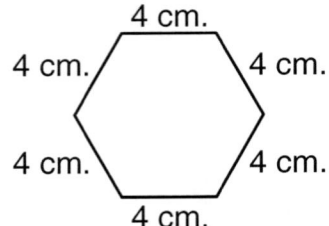

4 cm.

4 cm. 4 cm.

4 cm. 4 cm.

4 cm.

Ⓐ 11 cm

Ⓑ 12 cm

Ⓒ 20 cm

Ⓓ 24 cm

5. Continue the pattern.

540, 550, 560,

570, ____, ____, ____

Ⓐ 560, 550, 540

Ⓑ 570, 580, 590

Ⓒ 580, 590, 600

Ⓓ 580, 590, 610

6. Complete each of the fact families.

4 + 2 = 6   8 + 7 = 15   10 + 8 = 18

_____   _____   _____

_____   _____   _____

_____   _____

#51556—TIME For Kids: Practicing for Today's Tests

Practice Exercise 20 *(cont.)*

Directions: Read and solve each problem carefully.

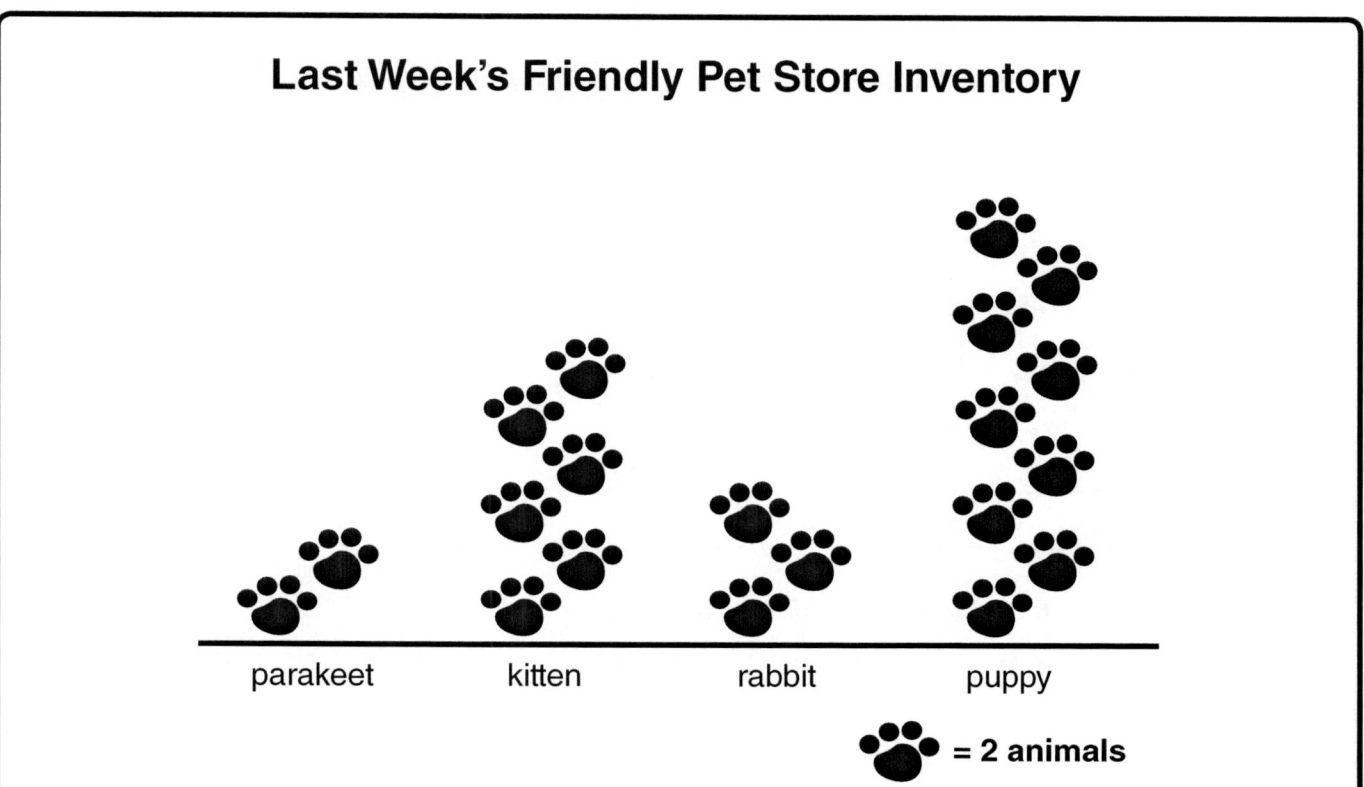

Last Week's Friendly Pet Store Inventory

parakeet   kitten   rabbit   puppy

= 2 animals

7. How many more puppies than rabbits are at the pet store?

Ⓐ 3

Ⓑ 6

Ⓒ 9

Ⓓ 12

8. What is the most common pet at the Friendly Pet Store?

Ⓔ kitten

Ⓕ puppy

Ⓖ rabbit

Ⓗ parakeet

Practice Exercise 20 (cont.)

Directions: Read and solve each problem carefully.

9. This week, the Friendly Pet Store received twice as many animals as last week. Use this information to fill in the chart with the new data.

This Week's Friendly Pet Store Inventory	
Animal	**Amount**
parakeet	
kitten	
rabbit	
puppy	

10. Use the information from the chart to create a picture graph showing how many animals are in the Friendly Pet Store this week. Make sure to include a title, a scale, labels, and a key.

Key = _____

Practice Exercise 21

Directions: Read and solve each problem carefully.

1. Which number makes the number sentence true?

   $$6 + 6 = 12 + \square$$

   Ⓐ 0

   Ⓑ 1

   Ⓒ 6

   Ⓓ 12

2. Arianna has 12 teddy bears. She gets 6 more teddy bears. About how many teddy bears does Arianna have now?

   Ⓐ 5

   Ⓑ 10

   Ⓒ 15

   Ⓓ 20

3. Elizabeth thinks these two shapes are both divided in fourths. Her friend Nicole disagrees. Explain who you agree with using words and numbers.

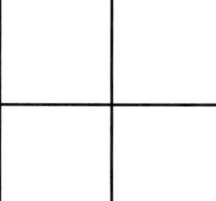 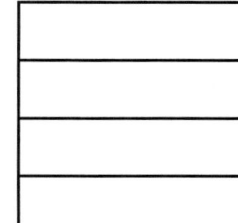

_____

_____

Practice Exercise 21 *(cont.)*

Directions: Read and solve each problem carefully.

4. Billy's team scored 75 points during their basketball game. Sam's team scored 63 points. How many fewer points did Sam's team score?

   (A) 8   (C) 122

   (B) 12   (D) 138

5. Which numbers will complete this pattern?

12, 15, _____, _____, 24

What is the pattern?

_____

_____

6. Using your ruler, draw and label these 3 triangles.

- Draw a triangle with sides that are all the same length.
- Draw a triangle with **two** sides that are the same length.
- Draw a triangle with sides that are **all** different lengths.

Practice Exercise 21 *(cont.)*

Directions: Read and solve each problem carefully.

Second Grade Field Trip to the Zoo

Class	Number of Teachers	Number of Students	Number of Chaperones
1	1	24	6
2	1	25	6
3	2	23	6
4	1	24	6

7. Each school bus holds 40 people. How many buses will be needed to take just the students to the zoo?

   Ⓐ 1

   Ⓑ 2

   Ⓒ 3

   Ⓓ 4

8. How many buses are needed to take the students, teachers, and chaperones to the zoo?

   Ⓔ 3

   Ⓕ 4

   Ⓖ 5

   Ⓗ 6

Name: _____ Date: _____

Practice Exercise 21 *(cont.)*

Directions: Read and solve each problem carefully.

9.

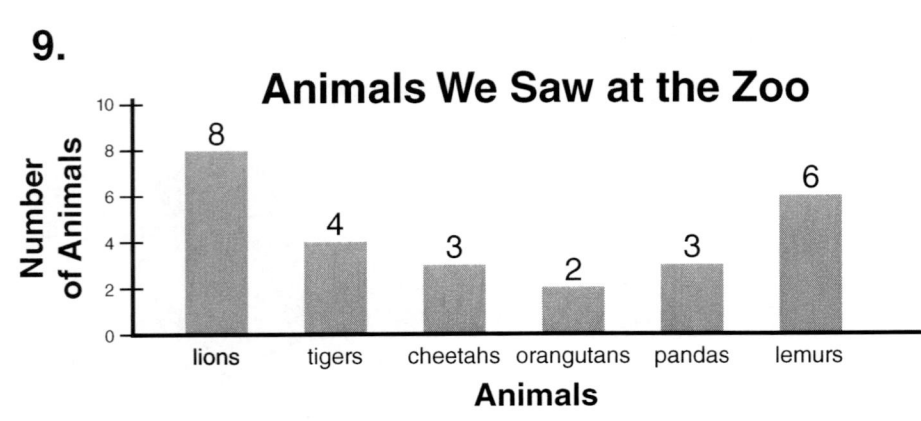

Animals We Saw at the Zoo

Create a line plot of the animals the students saw at the zoo. Use an X to represent each zoo animal.

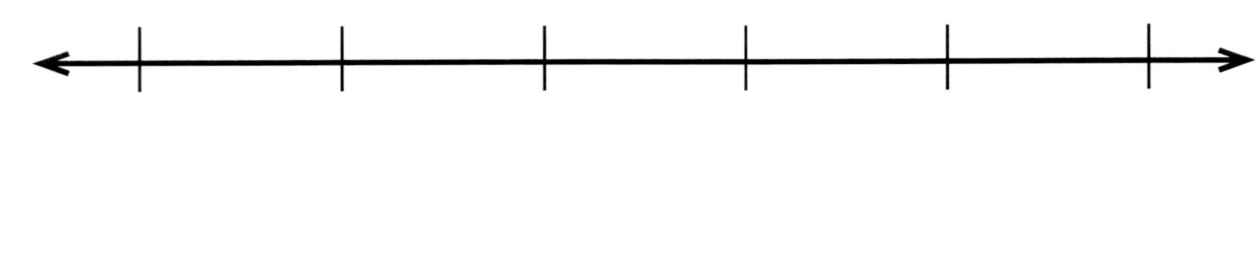

_____

10. Which animal did the students see the least? _____

Which animal did the students see the most? _____

Practice Exercise 22

Directions: Read and solve each problem carefully.

Four classes are going on a field trip. This chart shows some information about the trip.

Class	Numbers of Students	Number of Teachers	Number of Chaperones
1	22	2	5
2	24	1	6
3	24	1	6
4	23	1	5

1. How many total people are going on the field trip?

    Ⓐ 110   Ⓒ 124

    Ⓑ 120   Ⓓ 130

2. One bus holds 50 people. How many **full** buses will be needed for the field trip?

    Ⓔ 2

    Ⓕ 3

    Ⓖ 4

    Ⓗ 5

3. How many people will be in the unfilled bus?

_____

Write an equation to show how many more people can fit on this bus.

_____

Name: _____ Date: _____

Practice Exercise 22 (cont.)

Directions: Read and solve each problem carefully.

---

4. How many edges are in this shape?

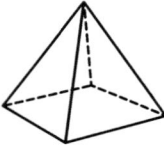

- Ⓐ 6
- Ⓑ 8
- Ⓒ 10
- Ⓓ 12

---

5. Which symbol makes the comparison true?

$$8 + 3 \; \boxed{} \; 4 + 5$$

- Ⓐ ×
- Ⓑ =
- Ⓒ <
- Ⓓ >

---

6. Julia wrote all the times for the events of the school fair on cards. She put the cards in her backpack, but they got out of order. Use the chart to create a schedule of all the events, putting them in order from 9:00 A.M. to 2:30 P.M.

Cake Walk 9:00 A.M.
Apple Bobbing 12:00 P.M.
Dunk Tank 2:30 P.M.
Cotton Candy Making 9:30 A.M.
Pin the Tail on the Donkey 1:30 P.M.
Piñata 11:00 A.M.
Bingo 12:30 P.M.
Relay Race 11:30 A.M.
Face Painting 1:00 P.M.
Water Balloon Toss 10:30 A.M.
Ring Toss 2:00 P.M.
Bean Bag Toss 10:00 A.M.

School Fair

Practice Exercise 22 *(cont.)*

Directions: Read and solve each problem carefully.

Mr. Steven's Class Rug

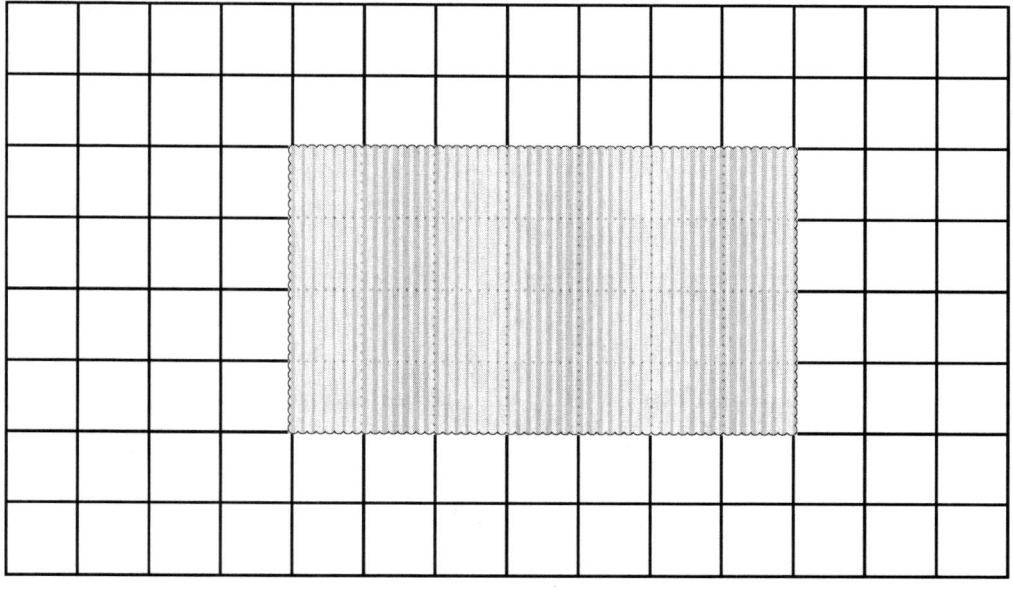

☐ = one square foot

---

7. What is the perimeter of this rug?

_____

8. What is the area of this rug?

_____

Practice Exercise 22 (cont.)

Directions: Read and solve each problem carefully.

---

9. A room that is 100 feet wide and 200 feet long can hold 50 people. Mr. Stevens has 27 students in his class. What is the **maximum** number of guests the students can invite to the class party?

_____

---

10. Each student at the party will be given two goody bags. How many bags will Mr. Stevens need to buy for his students?

_____

---

11. Mr. Stevens has to cover the floors and walls for protection during the party. How large is the perimeter of the room?

perimeter = _____

Practice Exercise 23

Directions: Read and solve each problem carefully.

1. How much money is shown?

Ⓐ $1.94   Ⓑ $1.99   Ⓒ $2.00   Ⓓ $2.04

2. Which shows 483 written in words?

Ⓐ four-eight-three hundred

Ⓑ forty-eight hundred three

Ⓒ four-eight-three hundred

Ⓓ four hundred eighty-three

3. Is 76 an even number or odd number? Explain how you know. Use words, numbers, or pictures to explain your thinking.0

_____

_____

_____

Name: _____ Date: _____

Practice Exercise 23 (cont.)

Directions: Read and solve each problem carefully.

---

4. Which two shapes have 6 faces?

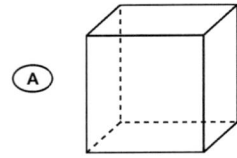
Ⓐ

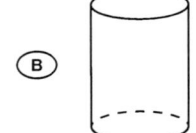
Ⓑ

Ⓒ

Ⓓ
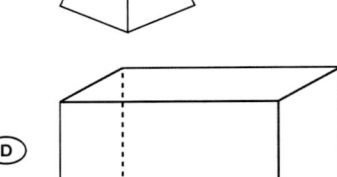

---

5. Write these numbers in order from least to greatest.

188, 137, 131, 152, 102, 190

_____

---

6. Nicholas starts his homework at 4:15. He does math for 15 minutes, spelling for 15 minutes, and reading for 30 minutes. Draw the hands on each clock to show the time Nicholas started his homework and the time he finished.

Start  Finish

---

Name: _____   Date: _____

Practice Exercise 23 *(cont.)*

Directions: Read and solve each problem carefully.

Supply List for Mrs. Thompson's Class
4 folders
4 composition books
1 pack of markers
1 box of crayons
2 packs of lined paper
2 packs of pencils (12 in a pack)
1 pair of scissors
6 glue sticks

7. Which item do students need the most of?

    Ⓐ folders

    Ⓑ pencils

    Ⓒ glue sticks

    Ⓓ composition books

8. How many pencils do students need to bring?

    Ⓔ 2

    Ⓕ 14

    Ⓖ 24

    Ⓗ 26

Practice Exercise 23 *(cont.)*

Directions: Read and solve each problem carefully.

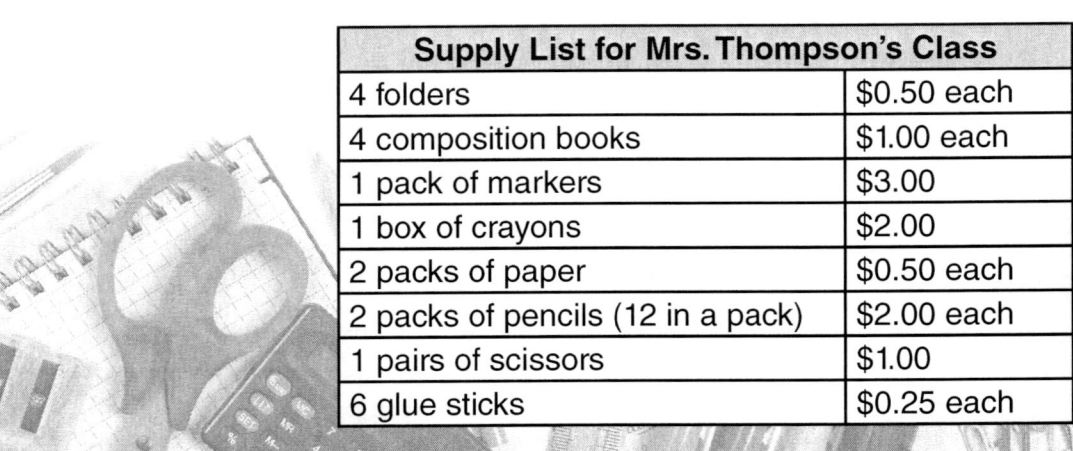

Supply List for Mrs. Thompson's Class	
4 folders	$0.50 each
4 composition books	$1.00 each
1 pack of markers	$3.00
1 box of crayons	$2.00
2 packs of paper	$0.50 each
2 packs of pencils (12 in a pack)	$2.00 each
1 pairs of scissors	$1.00
6 glue sticks	$0.25 each

9. How much will it cost to purchase all of the items?

_____

10. William gives the clerk $20.00 to pay for his supplies. How much change will he get back?

_____

Practice Exercise 24

Directions: Read and solve each problem carefully.

1. Jake has 10 trading cards. He gives away 5 trading cards. What fraction of his cards has Jake given away?

   Ⓐ $\frac{1}{5}$

   Ⓑ $\frac{1}{4}$

   Ⓒ $\frac{1}{3}$

   Ⓓ $\frac{1}{2}$

2. Which symbol makes the comparison true?

   756 ☐ 745

   Ⓐ >

   Ⓑ <

   Ⓒ =

   Ⓓ ×

3. Camila has 8 coins in her pocket. She has 77¢. List two combinations of coins she could have.

Practice Exercise 24 (cont.)

Directions: Read and solve each problem carefully.

---

4. What time is on the clock?

ⓐ 6:00   ⓒ 12:06

ⓑ 6:12   ⓓ 12:30

---

5. Hailey has 2 dozen markers. She gives her little sister 8 markers. How many markers does Hailey have left?

ⓐ 6

ⓑ 10

ⓒ 12

ⓓ 16

---

6. Each square on this graph paper has an area of 1 cm. Shade some of the squares to create a shape. Make sure to shade complete squares. What is the area of the shape you created? What is the perimeter of the shape you created?

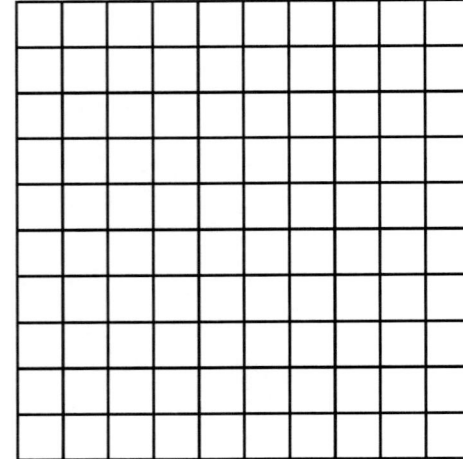

Scale

☐ = 1 cm

perimeter = _____

Practice Exercise 24 (cont.)

Directions: Read and solve each problem carefully.

Emma's Busy Day	
School	9:00 A.M.–4:00 P.M.
Snack	4:00 P.M.–4:15 P.M.
Take out the Trash	4:15 P.M.–4:30 P.M.
Piano Lesson	4:30 P.M.–5:00 P.M.
Homework	5:00 P.M.–5:30 P.M.
Dinner	5:30 P.M.–6:00 P.M.
Soccer	6:00 P.M.–7:30 P.M.
Playtime	7:30 P.M.–8:00 P.M.
Bedtime	8:00 P.M.

7. Which after-school activity lasts the longest?

  Ⓐ dinner

  Ⓑ soccer

  Ⓒ school

  Ⓓ homework

8. How many hours does Emma spend at school?

  Ⓔ 3

  Ⓕ 5

  Ⓖ 7

  Ⓗ 8

Practice Exercise 24 *(cont.)*

Directions: Read and solve each problem carefully.

9. On Thursday, Emma doesn't have piano lessons or soccer practice. Instead, she has lacrosse practice from 4:30–6:00 P.M. Create a schedule for Emma's day on Thursday.

Emma's Busy Thursday	

10. How long does lacrosse practice last?

_____

11. On Thursday, how many hours pass between when Emma arrives at school and her bedtime?

_____

Practice Exercise 25

Directions: Read and solve each problem carefully.

---

1. Which **two** shapes show $\frac{1}{4}$?

   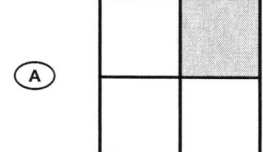 A   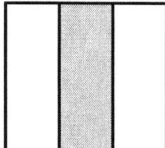 B    C   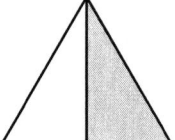 D

---

2. Luke has these coins in his pocket. He wants to buy a snack for a dollar. How much more money does he need to equal one dollar?

   A 8¢   C 18¢

   B 15¢   D 28¢

---

3. Use words, numbers, or pictures to explain why 954 is larger than 863.

   _____

   _____

   _____

Practice Exercise 25 (cont.)

Directions: Read and solve each problem carefully.

4. How many of the shapes shown have 4 sides and 4 right angles?

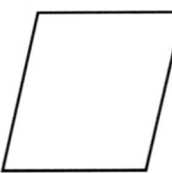 

   Ⓐ 1

   Ⓑ 2

   Ⓒ 3

   Ⓓ 4

5. Which expression shows 347 written in expanded form?

   Ⓐ 3 + 47

   Ⓑ 3 + 4 + 7

   Ⓒ 30 + 40 + 7

   Ⓓ 300 + 40 + 7

6. Write these numbers in order from least to greatest.

thirty-seven, eighty-two, fifty-five, eighteen

_____ _____ _____ _____

Practice Exercise 25 *(cont.)*

Directions: Read and solve each problem carefully.

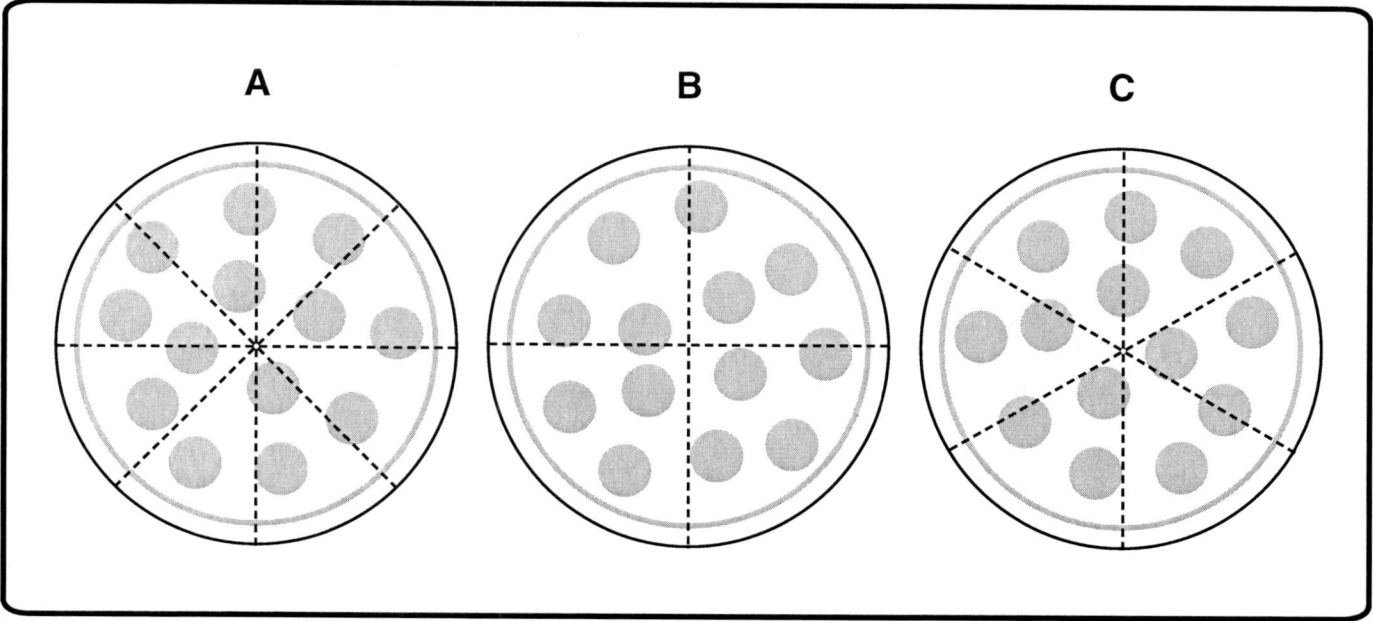

A   B   C

7. Which pizza has the largest size slices? How do you know?

_____

_____

_____

_____

8. Which pizza has the smallest slices? How do you know?

_____

_____

_____

_____

_____

Practice Exercise 25 (cont.)

Directions: Read and solve each problem carefully.

9. Mrs. Johnson ordered 3 pizzas for a class party. She wants each of her 24 students to have one slice of pizza. Divide these pizzas to make enough equal slices for her students.

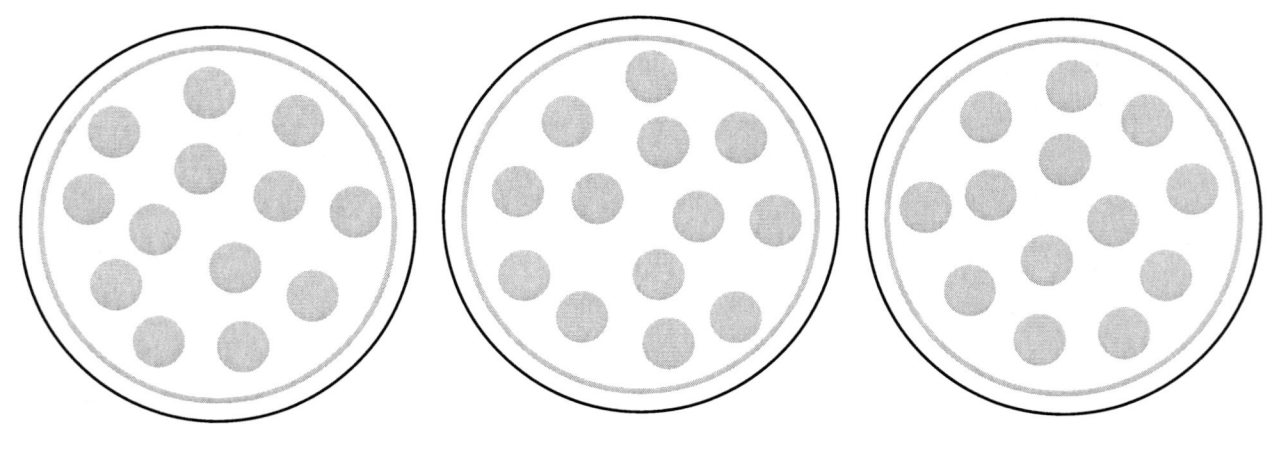

10. What fraction of a pizza is one slice?

11. How many slices equal one-half of a pizza?

References Cited

Ginsburg, Alan, Geneise Cooke, Steve Leinwand, Jay Noell, and Elizabeth Pollack. 2005. *Reassessing U.S. International Mathematics Performance: New Findings from the 2003 TIMSS and PISA*. Washington DC: American Institute for Research.

Ginsburg, David. 2014. "Support CCSS Math with Answer-Giving, Not Answer-Getting." *Education Week Teacher* http://blogs.edweek.org/teachers/coach_gs_teaching_tips/2014/07/support_math_ccss_with_answer-giving_not_answer-getting.html.

Leinwand, Steven, Daniel J. Brahier, and DeAnn Huinker. 2014. *Principles to Actions: Ensuring Mathematical Success For All.* Reston, VA: National Council of Teachers of Mathematics.

National Council of Teachers of Mathematics. 1989. *Curriculum and Evaluation Standards for School Mathematics*. Reston, VA: National Council of Teachers of Mathematics.

National Council of Teachers of Mathematics. 2000. *Principles and Standards for School Mathematics*. Reston, VA: National Council of Teachers of Mathematics.

National Council of Teachers of Mathematics. 2006. *Curriculum Focal Points for Prekindergarten through Grade 8 Mathematics.* Reston, VA: National Council of Teachers of Mathematics.

National Governors Association Center for Best Practices, Council of Chief State School Officers. 2010. Common Core Standards. National Governors Association Center for Best Practices, Council of Chief State School Officers: Washington D.C. http://www.corestandards.org.

National Research Council. 2001. *Adding It Up: Helping Children Learn Mathematics*. Washington DC: The National Academies Press.

O'Connell, Susan, and John SanGiovanni. 2013. *Putting the Practices Into Action.* Portsmouth, NH: Heinemann.

Rinehart, Steven C. 2000. "Never Say Anything a Kid Can Say!" *Mathematics Teaching in the Middle School.* 5 (8): 478–483.

Schmidt, William H., Curtis C. McKnight, and Senta A. Raizen. 1997. *A Splintered Vision: An Investigation of U.S. Science and Mathematics Education*. Heidelberg, Germany: Springer Science + Business Media.

Student Achievement Partners. 2013. *Achieve the Core.* Student Achievement Partners: New York. http://achievethecore.org.

Van de Walle, John A., Karen S. Karp, LouAnn H. Lovin, and Jennifer M. Bay-Williams. 2014. *Teaching Student-Centered Mathematics: Developmentally Appropriate Instruction for Grades 3–5.* Upper Saddle River, NJ: Pearson.

Question Types

The following chart correlates each question in this book to the mathematical strands. For more information on each mathematical strand, see page 7.

Unit	Question	Number & Operations in Base Ten	Number & Operations Fractions	Measurement, Money, Data, and Time	Geometry
1	1		X		
	2	X			
	3			X	
	4–6		X		
	7, 8			X	
	9–11		X		
2	1–4		X		
	5				X
	6–8			X	
	9–11		X		
3	1,2			X	
	3–5		X		
	6				X
	7–11			X	
4	1			X	
	2	X			
	3–5		X		
	6	X			
	7–10			X	
5	1–3			X	
	4		X		
	5				X
	6		X		
	7–10			X	
6	1				X
	2			X	
	3		X		
	4	X			
	5, 6		X		
	7–10			X	

Question Types (cont.)

Unit	Question	Number & Operations in Base Ten	Number & Operations Fractions	Measurement, Money, Data, and Time	Geometry
7	1			X	
	2–4		X		
	5				X
	6		X		
	7, 8			X	
	9, 10		X		
8	1				X
	2–4		X		
	5–10			X	
9	1–3		X		
	4			X	
	5		X		
	6				X
	7, 8			X	
	9–11		X		
10	1–4		X		
	5	X			
	6	X			X
	7–8			X	
	9, 10		X	X	
	11		X		
11	1, 2		X		
	3			X	
	4				X
	5			X	
	6		X		
	7		X	X	
	8			X	
	9–11		X		
12	1–3		X		
	4			X	
	5		X		
	6				X
	7, 8		X	X	
	9			X	
	10		X		

Question Types (cont.)

Unit	Question	Number & Operations in Base Ten	Number & Operations Fractions	Measurement, Money, Data, and Time	Geometry
13	1		X		
	2			X	
	3–6		X		
	7–10			X	
	11		X		
14	1			X	
	2		X		
	3				X
	4–6		X		
	7			X	
	8		X	X	
	9–10			X	
15	1–4		X		
	5				X
	6–11			X	
16	1–3		X		
	4			X	
	5, 6		X		
	7–11		X	X	
17	1, 2		X		
	3			X	
	4				X
	5, 6			X	
	7–10		X	X	
	11		X		
18	1, 2			X	
	3, 4		X		
	5				X
	6		X		
	7, 8			X	
	9–11		X	X	
19	1	X			
	2				X
	3	X			
	4		X		
	5–8			X	
	9–10		X		

Question Types *(cont.)*

Unit	Question	Number & Operations in Base Ten	Number & Operations Fractions	Measurement, Money, Data, and Time	Geometry
20	1		X		
	2			X	
	3		X		
	4				X
	5, 6		X		
	7–9			X	
	10		X	X	
21	1–5		X		
	6				X
	7, 8		X	X	
	9–10			X	
22	1–3		X	X	
	4				X
	5		X		
	6			X	
	7, 8			X	
	9–11		X		
23	1			X	
	2	X			
	3		X		
	4				X
	5	X			
	6–8			X	
	9–10		X	X	
24	1, 2		X		
	3, 4			X	
	5		X		
	6			X	
	7–11		X	X	
25	1		X		
	2			X	
	3	X			
	4				X
	5, 6	X			
	7–11		X		

Top Tips: Preparing for Today's Tests

Ways to Build Mathematical Thinking at Home

	TIME Time with adults is the first step! Checking in for a few minutes as your child works on homework will give you a great idea of what is going on at school.
	IDEAS Ask your child's teacher what the four or five "big ideas" of the year will be in math so you know what to support at home.
	MULTI-STEP and MULTI-ANSWER Be aware that many of today's word problems have multiple steps and sometimes more than one correct answer.
	ENVIRONMENT Set up a quiet place for at-home study where your child can concentrate without distractions.
	FIND As a family, find examples of math in the news, such as temperature changes. Having your child compare these numbers shows real-life applications of math.
	OPPORTUNITIES Make opportunities for using math at home, such as doubling recipes, making change, balancing a checkbook, and reading a clock.
	REVIEW Review by using specific prompts such as, "Name the most challenging problem you did in math this week." Or, "What is your favorite math tool to use?"
	KEEP Keep a positive math outlook! Instead of commenting, "I was never any good at math," assure your child that even if math is challenging, there are supports available at home and at school.
	INTERNET The Internet has many free and engaging math games. Just ten minutes of practice per day can help reinforce skills and yield long-term results.
	DIRECTIONS Having your child repeat directions in their own words is a clarifying activity when approaching a math task.
	SHARE Share with your child how you used math during your day to solidify its importance.

Top Tips: Preparing for Today's Tests *(cont.)*

Ways to Succeed During Mathematical Tests

	THINK Think about what the problem is saying and asking you to do.
	INFORMATION Carefully examine the information given in the problem, such as numbers, graphs, and/or charts.
	MULTI-STEP and MULTI-ANSWER Many word problems have several steps, and more than one answer may be correct.
	ELIMINATE Eliminate any multiple-choice responses that you know cannot be correct based on logical reasoning.
	FIX Fixing and adjusting your thinking is a part of math. If a problem-solving approach does not work, learn from it, and try again.
	OPERATIONS Choose the best operation to solve the problem. Prove your work with words, numbers, and/or pictures.
	READ Read and re-read carefully to be sure you understand the task. Read and re-read your own work to be sure it is complete and makes sense.
	KEEP IT POSITIVE Keep a positive math outlook! When facing a math challenge, perhaps you can do part of the problem, if not the entire problem. Or maybe you can skip a part for now and come back to it later. A positive attitude helps you work through solutions that do not come quickly.
	I DON'T GET IT "I don't get it" is NOT a question! Ask specific questions about specific parts of a math challenge in class, and ask about directions you do not understand.
	DIRECTIONS Directions are there for a reason. Read them carefully, and check each one off as you complete it.
	STRATEGIES You know them; now use them! Use strategies such as work backward, guess and check, make a table/chart/list, and draw a picture to help solve problems.

Mathematics Tools

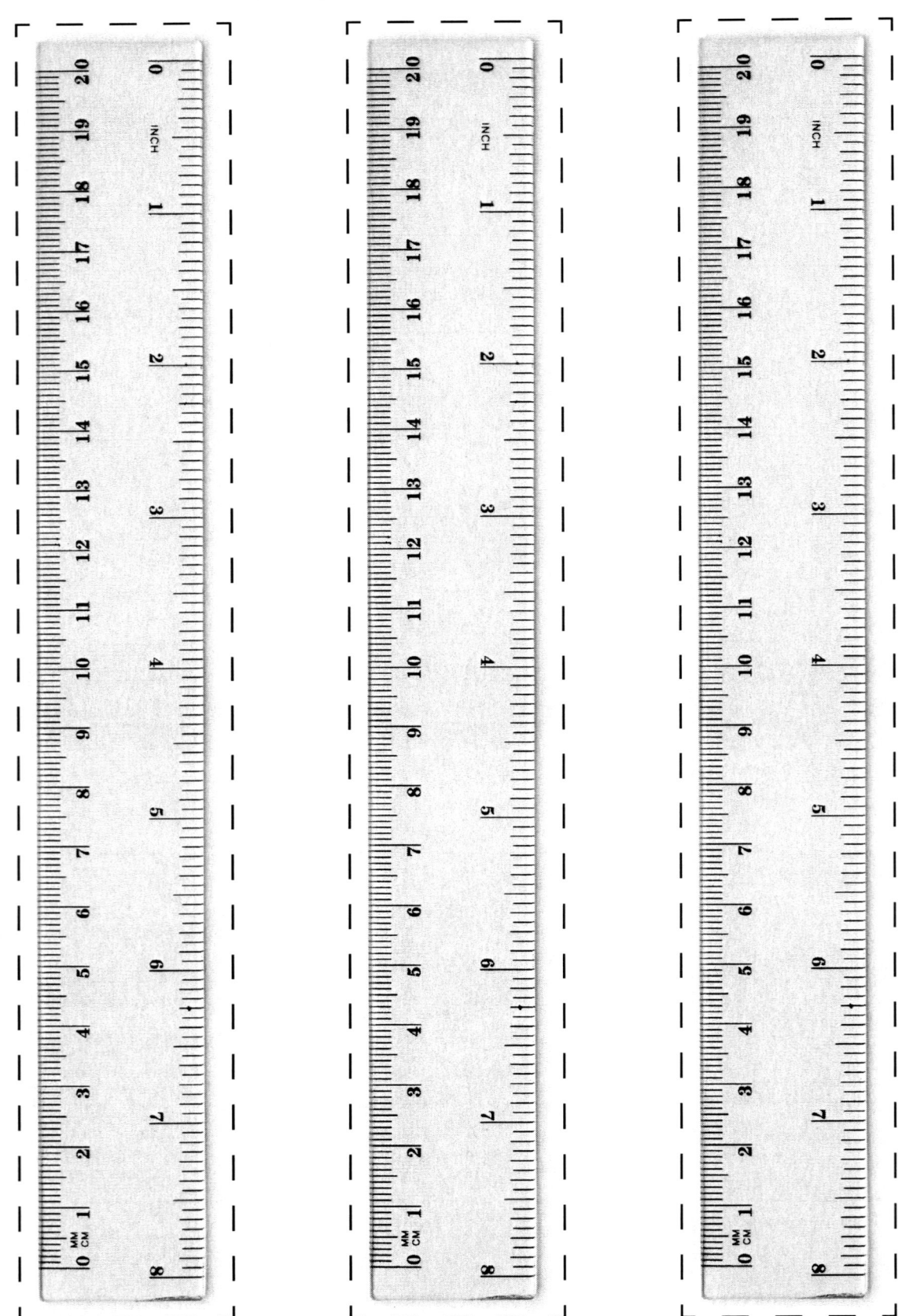

Mathematics Tools (cont.)

Length

1 foot = 12 inches

1 yard = 3 feet

1 meter = 100 centimeters

1 centimeter = 10 millimeters

Answer Key

Practice Exercise 1 (pages 13–16)

1. B. 15
2. D. 700 + 40 + 8
3. The graph is worth 4 points; give 1 point for each of the following: title, correct labels (x-axis and y-axis), scale, and correct representation of data.
4. A. >
5. C. 5
6. Possible answers might include: Amir's thinking is not correct because this flag would need to be divided into two equal pieces.
7. B. 5
8. F. 23
9. Students display 2 arrays equal to 30. Possible answers might include: 2 rows by 15, 6 rows by 5, 10 rows by 3.
10. 10 groups
11. 5 students

Practice Exercise 2 (pages 17–20)

1. B. 11
2. G. 3
3. Possible answers might include: 3 + 3 + 3 + 3 = 12; 3 × 4 = 12
4. B. 9
5. B. 6
6. 4:40
7. C. 8
8. Amirah is correct. Students should give relevant explanation with an understanding of rounding and/or estimation. Possible answers might include rounding 240 suckers on each arm to 200 or 250; when estimating the 8 arms this will result in an answer equal to (at least) 1,600 suckers.
9. Students show or explain that adding two even numbers will produce an answer that is always even.
10. Students show or explain that adding one even number and one odd number will produce an answer that is always odd.
11. Students show or explain that adding two odd numbers will produce an answer that is always even.

Practice Exercise 3 (pages 21–24)

1. D. more likely
2. F. less likely
3. $\frac{3}{4}$ is not stripped
4. C. 35
5. D. 36
6. Students should draw a square and a rectangle.

7. D. 2027
8. H. 2020
9. June 20
10. Thursday
11. Wednesday

Practice Exercise 4 (pages 25–28)

1. C. 7
2. C. 40
3. Check for understanding that the numerator indicates the number of sections colored and the denominator indicates the total number of sections. Possible answers might include:

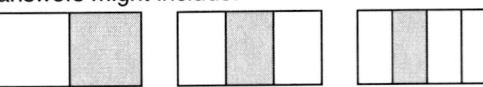

4. B. 8 + 7; D. 10 + 5
5. 9 apples
6. 1,000 + 200 + 60 + 4
7. A. 9–11 hours
8. G. 10 hours
9.

Animal	Number of Animals	Total Legs
cats	2	8
dog	1	4
fish	2	0
birds	3	6

10. The bar graph is worth 4 points; give 1 point for each of the following: title, correct labels (x-axis and y-axis), an appropriate scale, and correct representation of data.

Practice Exercise 5 (pages 29–32)

1. D. 4:45 P.M.
2. G.
3. 3 cm, 4 cm, 5 cm, 7 cm
4. C. 35, 50
5. B. circle
6. 48 laps
7. C. 100
8. G. 240 feet
9. 10 cm taller
10. The bar graph is worth 4 points, 1 point for each of the following: title, correct labels (x-axis and y-axis), an appropriate scale, and correct representation of data.

Answer Key *(cont.)*

Practice Exercise 6 (pages 33–36)

1. C. 8
2. C. $1.78
3. Possible answers might include: 23 + 13 − 6 = 30; 23 + 7 = 30
4. B. 80; C. 8 tens
5. B. 8
6. 2, 4, 6, 8, 10, 12, 14, 16, 18; Possible answers might include:18 + 18 = 36; 2 × 18 = 36
7. C. 13 feet
8. G. 3–5 years
9. Aquarium B has a greater area for the octopus to swim around.
10. Aquarium A has a smaller perimeter; it will have a shorter distance to walk around.

Practice Exercise 7 (pages 37–40)

1. C. 65°F
2. C. 62
3. Grace ate the larger piece. Students should demonstrate an understanding of why $\frac{1}{4}$ is bigger than $\frac{1}{8}$. Sample answer: $\frac{1}{4}$ is equivalent to $\frac{2}{8}$, which is larger than $\frac{1}{8}$.
4. B. 9
5. D. 12
6. Answer: 823. Students should demonstrate two ways to solve the expression.
7. C. 5
8. G. 17
9.

Items	Cost	How many should he buy?	Total cost of item
hot dogs	$3.00	2	$6.00
hot dog buns	$4.00	3	$12.00
cookies	$2.00	2	$4.00
chip boxes	$6.00	1	$6.00
juice boxes	$2.00	3	$6.00

10. $34.00

Practice Exercise 8 (page 41 —44)

1. B. 5
2. B. 90

3.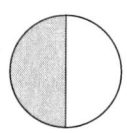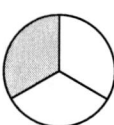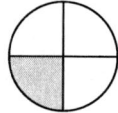

4. A. 4 + 8 = 12
5. C. 98¢
6. 2 inches, 5 centimeters. Centimeters are smaller units of measurement, so they will give you a larger number.
7. C. leatherback sea turtle
8. G. leatherback sea turtle
9. Nest 4
10. Nest 3

Practice Exercise 9 (pages 45–48)

1. B.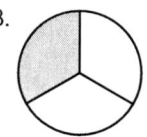

   D.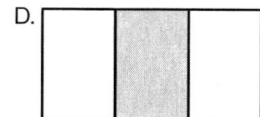

2. B. 21
3. 107
4. B. 18¢
5. A. 5 + 5; B. 6 + 4; D. 9 + 1
6. perimeter is 6 inches; possible answers might include: rectangle, kite, or parallelogram
7. A. wolf spider; B. goliath birdeater
8. F. huntsman spider
9. The problem is worth 3 points. Give 1 point for every correctly shaded shape.
10. Possible answers might include: the $\frac{1}{4}$ circle has the largest shaded part because $\frac{1}{4}$ is bigger than $\frac{1}{8}$.
11. The problem is worth 2 points. Students should give a rational explanation comparing $\frac{1}{2}$ to $\frac{1}{3}$.

Practice Exercise 10 (pages 49–52)

1. B. 9
2. D. 84 inches
3. 34 cherries; 8 + ☐ = 42 or 42 − 8 = ☐
4. C. 162; D. 170
5. D. 382
6. Shapes may vary; each shape has a perimeter of 12 cm.
7. C. Germany

Answer Key *(cont.)*

8. G. 3,000
9. 90 minutes or 1 horu and 30 minutes
10. 70 minutes or 1 hour and 10 minutes
11. 4 lawns = 2 hours before needing to be recharged

Practice Exercise 11 (pages 53–56)

1. A. <
2. B. 630
3. Kayla is incorrect. 12 hours have passed, as indicated by the change from the A.M. (morning) to P.M. (afternoon/evening).
4. A. cube; C. square pyramid
5. B. 2
6. 67. Students should demonstrate 2 ways of subtracting with an emphasis on place value.
7. C. 32
8. F. engineer
9. 75 minutes or 1 hour and 15 minutes
10. 5 copies/handouts/sheets of paper
11. 125 handouts/copies/sheets of paper

Practice Exercise 12 (pages 57–60)

1. A. >
2. C. 15
3. 163
4. A. 4 cm
5. B. 76
6. 5 faces; no, they are not all the same (1 square and 4 triangles)
7. D. 80,000
8. E. 5
9. Yes, because they are each divided into three equal parts.
10. No, because each section is not equal.

Practice Exercise 13 (pages 61–64)

1. D. 113
2. C. nickel
3. A total of 19 seashells fell out; 46 – ☐ = 27 or 46 – 27 = ☐
4. B. 17
5. D. $\frac{3}{4}$
6. 359 girls
7. C. Choctaw
8. F. Navajo
9. Students should draw a shape that includes 12 squares on the grid.

10. The perimeter will vary depending on the layout of the 12 square cm grid.
11. The perimeter would double because the area will be double.

Practice Exercise 14 (pages 65–68)

1. A.
2. B. 600, 300
3. Possible answers might include: square, rectangle, or trapezoid/rhombus
4. D. 24
5. B. >
6. She has 55¢; possible answers might include: 5, 10, 15, 20, 25, 30, 35, 40, 45, 50, 55 or 5 + 5 + 5 + 5 + 5 + 5 + 5 + 5 + 5 + 5 + 5; She needs 29 more nickels to buy the puzzle.
7. B. economy
8. E. 23
9. Sara earns $19.00 a week.
10. The bar graph is worth 4 points; 1 point for each of the following: title, correct labels (*x*-axis, and *y*-axis), an appropriate scale, and correct representation of data.

Practice Exercise 15 (pages 69–72)

1. A. 12
2. B. 6 + 7, C. 9 + 4
3. They raise $2,100
4. A. ⬤⬤⬤⬤⬤⬤◯◯
   B. ⬤⬤⬤◯
5. D. 4 centimeters
6. 30 minutes

Event	Time
language arts	9:00
lunch	11:00
math	11:30
recess	1:00
science	1:30
art	2:15
dismissal	3:00

7. C. Nebraska
8. H. Arkansas

Answer Key (cont.)

9. Bar graph is worth 4 points with a title, labels, and correct data: sunny = 4, raining = 1, cloudy = 2
10. 2 days
11. $\frac{2}{8}$ or $\frac{1}{4}$

Practice Exercise 16 (pages 73–76)

1. C. $100 - 64 = 36$
2. B. 78
3.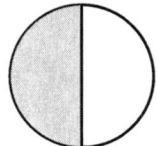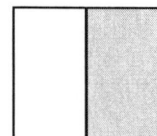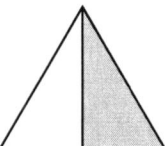
4. C. $1.62
5. C. 7
6. subtracting by ten
7. C. 25
8. G. 2006–2010
9. 37 more games
10. 475 games
11. 306 medals

Practice Exercise 17 (pages 77–80)

1. C. 97
2. B. 18
3. Possible answers might include: $4 + 4 + 8 + 6 = 22$ or $(2 + 2 + 4 + 3) \times 2 = 22$; 8 were sold on Friday
4. C. 17
5. B. yardstick
6. 15 minutes is one quarter of an hour.
7. A. 3
8. H. 28
9. 120 minutes
10. 1 hour and 15 minutes or 75 minutes
11. 2 hours and 30 minutes

Practice Exercise 18 (pages 81–84)

1. B. 4:45
2. G. 5:00
3. 387; $387 + 475 = 862$
4. B. 7
5. D. rectangle
6. Possible answers might include: $1 + 9$; $2 + 8$; $3 + 7$; $4 + 6$; $5 + 5$; $10 + 0$
7. 2 points if student labeled each section: blue = pizza, red/purple = hamburgers/burritos, yellow = peanut butter and jelly, green = salad bar

8. B. 20
9. 50 students
10. 13 boxes
11. 30 mangoes

Practice Exercise 19 (pages 85–88)

1. C.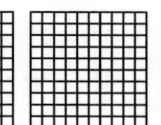
2. C. sphere
3. <
4. C. 24
5. D. 1 hour and 30 minutes
6. $1.98 - 78¢ = $1.20
7. C. 4
8. H. 16
9. new recipe: 3 pints of apple juice, 3 cups of orange juice, 3 cups of ginger ale
10. 6 cups

Practice Exercise 20 (pages 89–92)

1. C. 23
2. B. 97¢
3. They can each get 2 pieces.
4. D. 24 cm
5. C. 580, 590, 600
6. $2 + 4 = 6$, $6 - 4 = 2$, $6 - 2 = 4$; $7 + 8 = 15$, $15 - 8 = 7$, $15 - 7 = 8$; $8 + 10 = 18$, $18 - 10 = 8$, $18 - 8 = 10$
7. D. 12
8. F. puppy
9.

This Week's Friendly Pet Store Inventory	
Animal	Amount
parakeet	8
kitten	24
rabbit	12
puppy	36

10. The graph is worth 4 points; 1 point for each of the following: title, correct labels (x-axis and y-axis), scale, and correct representation of data.

Answer Key *(cont.)*

Practice Exercise 21 (pages 93–96)

1. A. 0
2. D. 20
3. Elizabeth is right. Both shapes are divided into four equal pieces.
4. B. 12
5. 18, 21; the pattern is counting/adding/increasing by 3
6. Drawings are worth 2 points—if student draws and labels three triangles (equilateral, isosceles, and scalene) correctly.
7. C. 3
8. F. 4
9. Line plot is worth 3 points; 1 point for each of the following: title, correct label, and data is accurately presented.
10. orangutan; lion

Practice Exercise 22 (pages 97–100)

1. B. 120
2. E. 2
3. 20; 20 + ? = 50 or 50 − 20 = ?
4. B. 8
5. D. >
6. School Fair:

Cake Walk at 9:00 A.M.
Cotton Candy Making at 9:30 A.M.
Bean Bag Toss at 10:00 A.M.
Water Balloon Toss at 10:30 A.M.
Piñata at 11:00 A.M.
Relay Race at 11:30 A.M.
Apple Bobbing at 12:00 P.M.
Bingo at 12:30 P.M.
Face Painting at 1:00 P.M.
Pin the Tail on the Donkey at 1:30 P.M.
Ring Toss at 2:00 P.M.
Dunk Tank at 2:30 P.M.

7. 22 feet
8. 28 square feet
9. 22 more guest
10. 54 bags
11. 20,000 ft² for the area; 600 feet for perimeter

Practice Exercise 23 (pages 101–104)

1. D. $2.04
2. D. four hundred eighty-three

3. It is even. Students should explain why it is even with an understanding of grouping and/or place value (the number in the ones place is 0, 2, 4, 6, or 8).
4. A. ; D.
5. 102, 131, 137, 152, 188, 190
6.
7. B. pencils
8. G. 24
9. $18.50
10. $1.50
11. Yes. William has $1.50, which is more than $1.25.

Practice Exercise 24 (pages 105–108)

1. D. $\frac{1}{2}$
2. A. >
3. Each combination should be equal to 77¢. Possible answers might include: 1 quarter, 5 dimes, 2 pennies; 1 half dollar, 5 nickels, 2 pennies
4. D. 12:30
5. D. 16
6. Answers should reflect the construction of the shape drawn.
7. B. soccer
8. G. 7 hours
9.

Emma's Busy Thursday	
school	9:00 A.M.–4:00 P.M.
snack	4:00 P.M.–4:15 P.M.
take out the trash	4:15 P.M.–4:30 P.M.
lacrosse practice	4:30 P.M.–6:00 P.M.
dinner	6:00 P.M.–6:30 P.M.
homework	6:30 P.M.–7:00 P.M.
playtime	7:00 P.M.–8:00 P.M.
bedtime	8:00 P.M.

10. 90 minutes or 1 hour and 30 minutes
11. 11 hours

Answer Key *(cont.)*

Practice Exercise 25 (pages 109–112)

1. A.

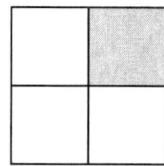

   C.

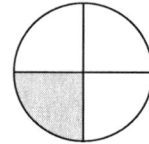

2. C. 18¢

3. Students should explain or compare the two numbers with a focus on place value.

4. B. 2

5. D. 300 + 40 + 7

6. eighteen, thirty-seven, fifty-five, eighty-two

7. Pizza B, because $\frac{1}{4}$ of a pizza has larger and fewer pieces, which means you get a larger piece.

8. Pizza A, because $\frac{1}{8}$ is the smallest fraction.

9. All three pizzas should be divided into eighths.

10. $\frac{1}{8}$

11. 4 slices

Notes